PSYCHOTHERAPY AND MATERIALISM

Cultural Inquiry

EDITED BY CHRISTOPH F. E. HOLZHEY
AND MANUELE GRAGNOLATI

The series 'Cultural Inquiry' is dedicated to exploring how diverse cultures can be brought into fruitful rather than pernicious confrontation. Taking culture in a deliberately broad sense that also includes different discourses and disciplines, it aims to open up spaces of inquiry, experimentation, and intervention. Its emphasis lies in critical reflection and in identifying and highlighting contemporary issues and concerns, even in publications with a historical orientation. Following a decidedly cross-disciplinary approach, it seeks to enact and provoke transfers among the humanities, the natural and social sciences, and the arts. The series includes a plurality of methodologies and approaches, binding them through the tension of mutual confrontation and negotiation rather than through homogenization or exclusion.

Christoph F. E. Holzhey is the Founding Director of the ICI Berlin Institute for Cultural Inquiry. Manuele Gragnolati is Professor of Italian Literature at the Sorbonne Université in Paris and Associate Director of the ICI Berlin.

PSYCHOTHERAPY AND MATERIALISM
Essays by François Tosquelles and Jean Oury

EDITED BY MARLON MIGUEL
AND ELENA VOGMAN

ISBN (Hardcover): 978-3-96558-080-0
ISBN (Paperback): 978-3-96558-081-7
ISBN (PDF): 978-3-96558-082-4
ISBN (EPUB): 978-3-96558-083-1

Cultural Inquiry, 31
ISSN (Print): 2627-728X
ISSN (Online): 2627-731X

Bibliographical Information of the German National Library
The German National Library lists this publication in the Deutsche Nationalbibliografie (German National Bibliography); detailed bibliographic information is available online at http://dnb.d-nb.de.

Cover design: Studio Bens. Film stills from Hélène Álvarez Tosquelles and François Tosquelles, *Société lozérienne d'hygiène mentale*, Institut Jean Vigo — Cinémathèque de Perpignan, 1954–57. Courtesy Michel Tosquelles.

In Europe, volumes are printed by Lightning Source UK Ltd., Milton Keynes, UK. See the final page for further details.

Digital editions can be viewed and downloaded freely at:
https://doi.org/10.37050/ci-31.

The volume is part of the project *Madness, Media, Milieus: Reconfiguring the Humanities in Postwar Europe*, funded by Volkswagen Foundation.

ICI Berlin Press is an imprint of
ICI gemeinnütziges Institut für Cultural Inquiry Berlin GmbH
Christinenstr. 18/19, Haus 8
D-10119 Berlin
publishing@ici-berlin.org
www.ici-berlin.org

Contents

Acknowledgments

This book would not have been possible without the collective efforts of individuals whose ethical, political, and intellectual engagement with the archives and legacies of institutional psychotherapy has ensured its transmission and continuation.

First and foremost, we extend our deepest thanks to Sophie Lesage, founder of Éditions d'une and French editor of numerous books by François Tosquelles and Jean Oury, among others.

We are immensely grateful to the Tosquelles family, particularly Jacques Tosquellas, for providing us with many unpublished manuscripts by François Tosquelles and for generously granting the rights to publish the translation of 'Psychopathology and Dialectical Materialism'. We also extend our thanks to Michel Tosquelles for providing us with the images from the film *Société lozérienne d'hygiène mentale* (Lozerien Society of Mental Hygiene).

Our special thanks goes to the family of Jean Oury, particularly Yannick Oury-Pulliero, for their trust and for granting us the rights to translate Oury's 'Institutional Psychotherapy: From Saint-Alban to La Borde'.

The contributions from Steven Corcoran, Anthony Faramelli, and Christian Scheerhorn in translation, research, and the processes of revision have been invaluable to this publication. We would also like to thank the devoted editorial team at ICI Berlin Press for their support, particularly Louisa Elderton, Manuele Gragnolati, Christoph Holzhey, and Claudia Peppel.

We too are grateful to Carles Guerra and Joana Masó for their foundational and stimulating curatorial and editorial work, which has significantly contributed to the transmission and visibility of institutional psychotherapy's extensive archives.

The pioneering work of artists such as Josephine Guattari, Angela Melitopoulos, and François Pain has revealed the concrete entanglements between image and word, act and speech, machine and subjectivity, aesthetics and ethics — all of which lie at the heart of institutional psychotherapy's praxis.

Finally, we would like to thank our collaborators Henning Schmidgen, who has consistently supported and encouraged our work at Bauhaus-Universität Weimar, and Matteo Pasquinelli, who first inspired the idea of translating the text by Tosquelles featured in this volume.

This book was produced with the generous support of the Freigeist Fellowship from the Volkswagen Foundation, which sponsors our research project, 'Madness, Media, Milieus: Reconfiguring the Humanities in Postwar Europe', at Bauhaus-Universität Weimar.

'Disalienation of the Total Fact of Madness'
An Introduction

MARLON MIGUEL AND ELENA VOGMAN

> Institutional psychotherapy is perhaps the act of setting up all kinds of mechanisms to fight, every day, against all that could turn the whole of the 'collective' toward a concentrationary or segregationist structure.
>
> Jean Oury, 1970

SITUATING INSTITUTIONAL PSYCHOTHERAPY

This book brings together two texts, both originally conceived as talks, belonging to the French psychiatric reform movement of 'institutional psychotherapy'. The first, 'Psychopathology and Dialectical Materialism',[1] was presented

---

1   This title was chosen by the French editor, Sophie Lesage. Tosquelles's original title was 'Psychopathology in Light of Dialectical Materialism', see also François Tosquelles, 'Psychopathology and Dialectical Materialism', in this volume, p. 47, note *.

in 1947 by Catalan psychiatrist François Tosquelles, director of Saint-Alban-sur-Limagnole psychiatric hospital in Central-Southern France, in the context of a lecture series on neurology and psychiatry at École normale supérieure in Paris. The second, 'Institutional Psychotherapy: From Saint-Alban to La Borde', was given by French psychiatrist Jean Oury — founder and director of La Borde clinic in Cour-Cheverny — in 1970 in Poitiers. These somewhat heterogeneous texts, formulated in distinct historical situations, are clear attempts at taking a stand in a conflictual epistemic and political sphere of psychiatric knowledge and practice. Both presentations testify to their authors' engagements not only in textual but also in oral transmission of their critical clinical experiences.[2] Such experiences aimed to transform psychiatric institutions and bring a new understanding of care practice involving social, environmental, and aesthetic realms. Against the dominant dehumanizing and devalorizing psychiatric practice of his time, Tosquelles claimed 'madness' to be crucially 'a human phenomenon', endowed with 'freedom, responsibility, and meaning'.[3]

Institutional psychotherapy — a term coined in 1952 by psychiatrists Georges Daumézon and Philippe Koechlin[4] — was a psychiatric reform and resistance movement.

---

2   Oury, for example, taught weekly seminars until just before he died. These were held at both La Borde (from 1971 onwards) and at Saint-Anne hospital in Paris (from 1981 onwards).

3   François Tosquelles, *Le Vécu de la fin du monde dans la folie. Le Témoignage de Gérard de Nerval* (Grenoble: Jérôme Millon, 2012), p. 98. Unless otherwise indicated, all translations in this introduction are the editors' own.

4   Georges Daumézon and Philippe Koechlin, 'La Psychothérapie institutionnelle française contemporaine', *Anais portugueses de psiquiatria*, 4.4 (1952), pp. 271–312. Georges Daumézon (1912–1979) was a French psychiatrist. He was medical director at Fleury-les-Aubrais psychiatric hospital from 1938 to 1951, where he initiated significant reforms in

It proposed a radical restructuring of clinical institutions by actively involving patients in these processes. While undertaking a Marxist rethinking of psychoanalysis, institutional psychotherapy also implemented *Gestalt* psychology and existential philosophy into clinical theory and practice. One of its main goals, as Oury points out, was to fight against forms of confinement that were 'concentrationary'[5] — a recurrent term used in the aftermath of World War II following the revelation of the crimes of

psychiatric care. Daumézon first met François Tosquelles in 1942 at a conference in Montpellier, marking the beginning of their collaborative work and his frequent visits to Saint-Alban (see *Histoire de la psychiatrie de secteur ou le secteur impossible?*, ed. by Lion Murard and François Fourquet, special issue of *Recherches*, 17 (1975), p. 109). In 1952, Daumézon and Philippe Koechlin (1938–2010), who was completing his specialist training in psychiatry with Daumézon, would coin the term 'institutional psychiatry' in one of the first articles offering an overview of the theoretical and historical backdrop, as well as the concrete changes the movement had introduced in psychiatric institutions in the post-war years. This seminal article, titled 'La Psychothérapie institutionnelle française contemporaine', was published in the *Anais Portugueses de Psiquiatria*, a journal edited by Hospital Júlio de Matos in Lisbon. In 1951, the journal started an exchange service with foreign publications, fostering an international dialogue in psychiatry, publishing titles in languages as diverse as German, Czech, Croatian, Spanish, Finnish, French, English, Italian, Japanese, Polish, Russian, and Portuguese (see 'História da Biblioteca', Centro Hospitalar Psiquiátrico de Lisboa, n. d., <https://www.chpl.min-saude.pt/servicos-de-apoio-geral/biblioteca/historia/> [accessed 23 June 2024]). According to Carlos De Brito, Daumézon and Koechlin's article did not find a publisher in France and was therefore published in the *Anais Portugueses de Psiquiatria* thanks to one of its editors, Barahona Fernandes (see Carlos De Brito, 'Jacques Postel, de loin et de près, *in memoriam*', *L'Information psychiatrique*, 99.2 (2023), p. 126). This fact reveals the difficulties of speaking critically about psychiatric conditions in post-war France.

5   See Jean Oury, 'Institutional Psychotherapy: From Saint-Alban to La Borde', in this volume, p. 91. In Daumézon's and Koechlin's formulation articulated in the aftermath of World War II, 'the comparison between the asylum world and the concentrationary universe inevitably imposes itself' (Daumézon and Koechlin, 'La Psychothérapie institutionnelle française contemporaine', pp. 282–83).

FIG. 1. Tearing down the walls of Saint-Alban. Film still from Hélène Álvarez Tosquelles and François Tosquelles, *Société lozérienne d'hygiène mentale* (Lozerien Society of Mental Hygiene), Institut Jean Vigo — Cinémathèque de Perpignan, 1954–57. Courtesy Michel Tosquelles.

FIG. 2. Tearing down the walls of Saint-Alban. Film still from Hélène Álvarez Tosquelles and François Tosquelles, *Société lozérienne d'hygiène mentale* (Lozerien Society of Mental Hygiene), Institut Jean Vigo — Cinémathèque de Perpignan, 1954–57. Courtesy Michel Tosquelles.

eugenics and concentration camps that describes psychiatry as a biopolitical and social regime of modern states and their dealings with confinement. Félix Guattari, who worked his entire life at La Borde, historically situated institutional psychotherapy as follows:

> After the prison camps and concentration camps, a few nurses and psychiatrists started to look at the problems of psychiatric hospitals from an entirely new angle. Incapable of supporting concentrationary institutions [*institutions concentrationnaires*], they undertook to transform services from top to bottom, knocking down fences and organizing the fight against famine. […] Surrealist intellectuals, doctors strongly influenced by Freudianism, and Marxist militants all mingled.[6]

The insight into the politics of confinement as entangled with social, mental, bodily, and spatial conditions led institutional psychotherapy to shift the focus in a crucial way: rather than an individual body needing treatment, it is the hospital as a form of warehousing bodies and institutional politics that requires attention. Institutional psychotherapy proposed that in order to adequately support individuals with psychic suffering, the primary step was to treat, heal, and care for the institution itself — *soigner l'institution* in French.[7]

The movement emerged at the Saint-Alban hospital in the Lozère department as a practice of resistance dur-

---

6   Félix Guattari, *Psychoanalysis and Transversality: Texts and Interviews 1955–1971*, trans. by Ames Hodges (Los Angeles: Semiotext(e), 2015), p. 60, the editors have slightly amended the translation; *Psychanalyse et transversalité. Essais d'analyse institutionnelle* (Paris: La Découverte, 2003), p. 39.

7   François Tosquelles, *Le Travail thérapeutique à l'hôpital psychiatrique* (Paris: Éditions du Scarabée, 1967), p. 41; republished as *Le Travail thérapeutique en psychiatrie* (Toulouse: Érès, 2015).

ing the German occupation and the fascist Vichy government. Today it is known that during this period between 40,000 and 80,000 patients of psychiatric institutions fell prey to the so-called 'soft extermination' policy.[8] As a way of resisting those measures of annihilation, which included a deficient diet and shortages of medication and clinical care, Saint-Alban became a collectively organized site of resistance and clandestine activities. To navigate the emergency years of the occupation, the patients were involved in different activities to provide alternative infrastructures of alimentation: these included gardening as well as foraging for pine cones and mushrooms in the forest, guided by the hospital's mushroom displays. The patients were also engaged in undertakings on nearby farms, contributing to the harvesting process. Hospital-based work included activities like sewing and knitting for local farmers. An informal bartering system emerged, offering creative communal solutions that overcame the severe shortages.[9] As a result, according to Dominique and Renée Mabin, Saint-Alban had the lowest mortality rate from starvation among French psychiatric hospitals: 'There was no *"extermination douce"*'.[10] Initiated by psychiatrists François Tosquelles, Lucien Bonnafé, André Chaurand, and André Clément, the movement was carried out

---

8   Max Lafont, *L'Extermination douce. La Cause des fous, 40 000 malades mentaux morts de faim dans les hôpitaux sous Vichy* (Lormont: Le Bord de l'Eau, 2000); Isabelle von Bueltzingsloewen, *L'Hécatombe des fous. La Famine dans les hôpitaux psychiatriques français sous l'Occupation* (Paris: Flammarion, 2009); Armand Ajzenberg, *L'Abandon à la mort... de 76000 fous par le régime de Vichy* and André Castelli, *Un hôpital psychiatrique sous Vichy (1940–1945)* (Paris: L'Harmattan, 2012).

9   Dominique and Renée Mabin, 'Art, folie et surréalisme à l'hôpital psychiatrique de Saint-Alban-sur-Limagnole pendant la guerre', *Mélusine*, 13 March 2015 <https://melusine-surrealisme.fr/wp/art-folie-et-surrealisme-a-lhopital-psychiatrique/> [accessed 30 March 2024].

10   Ibid.

FIG. 3. The camera is part of the collective construction
process at Saint-Alban, at which stones are being passed
from one person to the next. Film still from Hélène Álvarez
Tosquelles and François Tosquelles, *Société lozérienne
d'hygiène mentale* (Lozerien Society of Mental Hygiene),
Institut Jean Vigo — Cinémathèque de Perpignan, 1954–57.
Courtesy Michel Tosquelles.

Fig. 4. The camera is part of the collective construction
process at Saint-Alban, at which stones are being passed
from one person to the next. Film still from Hélène Álvarez
Tosquelles and François Tosquelles, *Société lozérienne
d'hygiène mentale* (Lozerien Society of Mental Hygiene),
Institut Jean Vigo — Cinémathèque de Perpignan, 1954–57.
Courtesy Michel Tosquelles.

FIG. 5. The camera observes the collective construction
process at Saint-Alban, at which stones are being passed
from one person to the next. Film still from Hélène Álvarez
Tosquelles and François Tosquelles, *Société lozérienne
d'hygiène mentale* (Lozerien Society of Mental Hygiene),
Institut Jean Vigo — Cinémathèque de Perpignan, 1954–57.
Courtesy Michel Tosquelles.

by a heterogeneous group comprised of surrealist artists, nuns from the Saint-Régis community, Jewish refugees, philosophers, and resistance fighters including Georges Canguilhem, Tristan Tzara, Jacques Matarasso, Paul Éluard and Nusch Éluard. This entangled pursuit of political resistance and mental 'disalienation' became key to institutional psychotherapy, which was later developed and transformed by authors such as Frantz Fanon, Félix Guattari, and Oury — all of whom spent a significant amount of time at Saint-Alban — as well as Anne Querrien, Ginette Michaud, Danielle Sivadon, Fernand Deligny, and others.

In the post-war period, institutional psychotherapy was further developed as a set of theoretical and practical interventions into the structure of the institution, operating at the intersection of environmental, medical, aesthetic, and social dimensions (Figures 1–5). It instituted a radically horizontal collective of patients, workers, and doctors, and developed media-therapeutic practices that aimed to transform the inner and outer milieus of psychic suffering. These milieu-oriented experiments were realized through an intense, multifaceted use of media such as the patient-run production of an intra-hospital newspaper titled *Trait-d'Union* (Figures 6–9), writing and theatre workshops, and filming, as well as the organization of ciné-clubs, carnivals (Figures 10–12), and other festivities welcoming the inhabitants of Lozère (Figure 13).

Despite taking a critical position with its social and political stance, institutional psychotherapy nonetheless embraced contemporary treatments of psychosis such as electroshock or insulin cure in its medical practice. Those 'inopportune and hybrid therapies'[11] — as critically re-

---

11   Antonin Artaud, 'Alienation and Black Magic', in *Artaud the Mômo*, ed. by Stephen Barber and trans. by Clayton Eshleman (Zurich/Berlin: Diaphanes, 2020), pp. 88–111 (p. 91).

ferred to by Antonin Artaud, artist and psychiatric patient of Rodez, who was also partly in Tosquelles's treatment — were a common intervention, which was accompanied by rehabilitation via social therapy. Tosquelles, Fanon, and later Oury and Guattari had positively theorized electroshock as a therapy of 'annihilation' induced by electricity, known also as 'Bini method', named after its Italian inventor, Professor Lucio Bini.[12]

Tosquelles's emphasis on 'activity' and activation of the patients was at the core of his clinical practice. These notions were inspired by Marxist theory — in particular the early Marx of *Theses on Feuerbach*, but also the *Economic and Philosophic Manuscripts* of 1844, extensively quoted in Tosquelles's text — and the insistence that knowledge is 'sensibly human activity, practice'.[13] The notion of 'activity' was also derived from the work of German psychiatrist Hermann Simon. Tosquelles's 'social therapy' — a term he used throughout the 1950s — was based on patients' activation, their participation in daily life at the hospital, and responsibility. It relied on Simon's *Aktivere Krankenbehandlung in der Irrenanstalt* (More Active Patient Treatment in the Mental Asylum), published in 1929. Tosquelles recalls having brought a copy of this book from Catalonia. At Saint-Alban, it was collectively translated into French, likely with reference to the Spanish translation of the book, and thanks in particular to the efforts of Eugénie Balvet. It

---

12   In an article co-authored by Tosquelles and Fanon, the question is to 'situate' the 'annihilation therapy through repeated shocks within an institutional therapeutic performance'. Frantz Fanon and François Tosquelles, 'On Some Cases Treated with the Bini Method', in Frantz Fanon, *Alienation and Freedom*, ed. by Jean Khalfa and Robert J. C. Young, and trans. by Steven Corcoran (London: Bloomsbury, 2018), pp. 285–90 (p. 285).

13   Tosquelles quoting Marx in 'Psychopathology and Dialectical Materialism', p. 56.

was then printed and circulated there in the 1940s. Whilst being the founder of modern work therapy, Simon embraced and supported ideas later propagated by the Nazi state, in particular those relating to social Darwinism: it was Tosquelles who transformed this theoretical impulse into a therapy of resistance and empowerment of the patients.[14]

Another reference, even prior to that of Simon, is Emilio Mira y López, who Tosquelles credits with completing the conceptualization of activity through his emphasis on the intimate relationship between bodily and muscular activity and social and mental activation. Mira y López was Professor of Psychiatry at the University of Barcelona, and a friend and close collaborator of Tosquelles at the psychiatric hospital Institut Pere Mata in Reus, Spain. Their joint

---

14   'Simon placed his concept [of more active patient treatment] within broader "biological" and psychological contexts, which were rooted in a biologistic-social Darwinist worldview. This worldview was also open to eugenic-racial hygiene ideas and a fundamental critique of welfare state provisions.' Bernd Walter, 'Hermann Simon — Psychiatriereformer, Sozialdarwinist, Nationalsozialist?', *Der Nervenarzt*, 73 (2002), pp. 1047–1054 (p. 1047). It is unknown whether Tosquelles knew about Simon's eugenic stance towards chronic psychiatric patients deemed unfit for work. Nonetheless, Tosquelles's socially and politically engaged psychiatric approach during World War II and in its aftermath was certainly the opposite of Simon's postulate of labour as 'education' of the patient. Within this framework, Simon fully aligned with the dramatic shift in health policies following the National Socialists' rise to power in 1933 and was even supportive of euthanasia practices: 'There was no significant distance between his conservative stance, his understanding of the state, his biologistic thinking, and his clear support for Hitler and Nazi racial policies.' (Ibid.) Simon's practices of labour as therapy were theorized and advanced by Carl Schneider, professor of psychiatry at the University of Heidelberg after the Nazis removed his predecessor from office. Schneider is known to have actively participated in *Aktion T4*, the Nazi regime's mass murder campaign targeting individuals deemed unfit or undesirable. In any case, in 1967, Tosquelles addressed a clear critique vis-à-vis Simon and Schneider's ideas, revealing their '"biology" of work' as 'leading directly or indirectly to murder', which was 'the case for the patients in Germany' (Tosquelles, *Le Travail thérapeutique à l'hôpital psychiatrique*, p. 38).

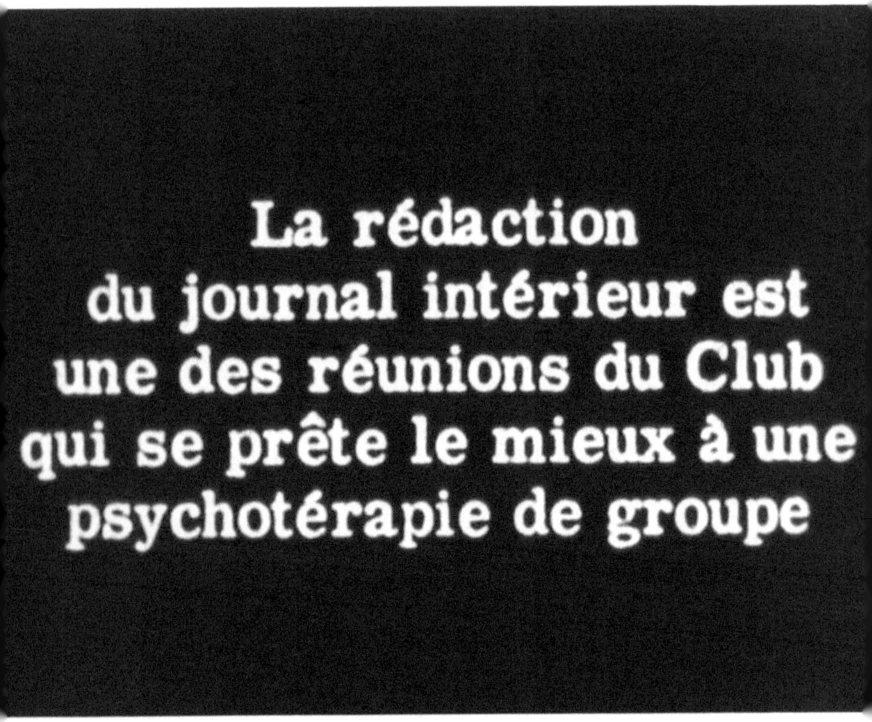

FIG. 6. 'Writing the internal newspaper is one of the Club's activities most suited to group psychotherapy.' Film still from Hélène Álvarez Tosquelles and François Tosquelles, *Société lozérienne d'hygiène mentale* (Lozerien Society of Mental Hygiene), Institut Jean Vigo — Cinémathèque de Perpignan, 1954–57. Courtesy Michel Tosquelles.

Fig. 7. A person, presumably a patient, is setting the
movable type for printing the intra-hospital newspaper titled
Trait-d'Union (Hyphen). Film still from Hélène Álvarez
Tosquelles and François Tosquelles, *Société lozérienne
d'hygiène mentale* (Lozerien Society of Mental Hygiene),
Institut Jean Vigo — Cinémathèque de Perpignan, 1954–57.
Courtesy Michel Tosquelles.

experiments developed into an 'extensive psychiatry': an expanded perspective of psychiatric care through the implementation of *Gestalt* psychology, psychotechnics, and psychoanalysis, which highlighted the agency of the body in the frame of 'occupational therapy'. Occupational therapy — or 'ergotherapy', the term Tosquelles generally uses and which refers to a different tradition — was practised at Pere Mata and relied on the conviction that 'the performance of new [bodily] movements would destroy the distorted patterns of muscular reaction that have become fixed and rigid in the individual, thus creating the possibility of the corresponding change in his frame of mind'.[15]

At Saint-Alban, the activation of patients through ergotherapy went hand in hand with the implementation of aesthetic practices and media that would enhance the social ties between patients, doctors, and nurses. In this way, the film 'Société lozérienne d'hygiène mentale' (Lozerien Society of Mental Hygiene) produced by François and Hélène Álvarez Tosquelles together with their patients between 1954 and 1957, presents the hospital as a 'society', a formation of resistance against the state-imposed conditions of confinement. Another more structural example of the hospital's activity was the 'Club', which was a central organ of the institution, independent from its administration, that was maintained by the patients. The Club was responsible for the hospital's social activities — such as ergotherapy sessions, the production of newspapers, or the organization of ciné-club sessions and festivities. As an 'institutional object',[16] the Club became a constant in

---

15 Emilio Mira y López, *Psychiatry in War* (New York: W. W. Norton & Company, 1943), also available online at <https://www.miraylopez.com/PsW_tot.html> [accessed 3 April 2024].

16 François Tosquelles, *Théorie et pratique de la psychothérapie institutionnelle*, in particular, Chap. 3: '"Objets institutionnels" ou "organismes

later clinical experiments in different settings of institutional psychotherapy, such as La Borde. It can be seen as an instrument of conviviality, enabling exchange among patients themselves, but also between patients, nurses, and the hospital's outside; it allowed for patients' autonomous decision-making and for a crucial de-hierarchization and multiplication of the relations between inmates and staff, 'doctor' and 'patient'.

INSTITUTIONAL PSYCHOTHERAPY'S LEGACIES

Institutional psychotherapy considered sociability, generated through activity, as the catalyst of its ecology of care. Again, when following a Marxist vision, social relations cannot be predetermined, but instead are situated and emerge in a complex environment co-constitutive of the singular individuals inhabiting it. In this sense, the very principle of institutional psychotherapy is its constant re-invention: reinvention of activities, structures, and forms of organization. If we can definitively identify a legacy of the Saint-Alban experiment, this would not be the simple reproduction of solidified principles, but their reinvention *in situ*, in a new context.

Two key examples can be cited that contributed to such a reinvention of institutional psychotherapy in a new

---

institutionnels" utiles et indispensables dans le champ de la psycho-thérapie institutionnelle' ('Institutional objects' or 'institutional organisms' useful and indispensable in the field of institutional psychotherapy), 1982, in Tosquelles Archives, organized by Jacques Tosquellas. By 'institutional object' or 'organism' Tosquelles means apparatuses invented and practised that have an 'instrumental function' in the psychiatric setting, helping to set up patients' activities and circulation. Tosquelles also mentions an idea of 'intermediary objects' to create these specific psychotherapeutic spaces. The idea is inspired by Winnicott's 'transitional objects'. The editors would like to thank Jacques Tosquellas for sharing with them this yet unpublished document.

FIG. 8. A person is reading a copy of *Trait d'Union*, Saint-Alban's internal newspaper. Film still from Hélène Álvarez Tosquelles and François Tosquelles, *Société lozérienne d'hygiène mentale* (Lozerien Society of Mental Hygiene), Institut Jean Vigo — Cinémathèque de Perpignan, 1954–57. Courtesy Michel Tosquelles.

FIG. 9. Poster production at Saint-Alban using movable type. Film still from Hélène Álvarez Tosquelles and François Tosquelles, *Société lozérienne d'hygiène mentale* (Lozerien Society of Mental Hygiene), Institut Jean Vigo — Cinémathèque de Perpignan, 1954–57. Courtesy Michel Tosquelles.

context: the clinic of La Borde, co-founded in 1953 by Oury in France, and Blida-Joinville hospital, directed by Frantz Fanon between 1953 and 1956 in the radically different climate of the anti-colonial war in Algeria. In both cases, an encounter with Tosquelles and an experience at Saint-Alban preceded these new constellations. For Oury, Tosquelles's lecture at École normale supérieure in 1947 — translated in this volume — gave him the impulse to join Saint-Alban that same year for an internship with psychiatrist Maurice Despinoy, who studied in Lyon. Only a few years later, after finishing his studies in medicine, also in Lyon, Fanon joined the same internship position alongside Despinoy at Saint-Alban, where he worked for fifteen months in close collaboration with Tosquelles between 1952 and 1953. There, he was responsible for the nurses' training in social therapy.

Upon his arrival at Blida-Joinville, Fanon implemented several changes modelled upon institutional psychotherapy: he set up a Club, built a soccer stadium and a theatre within the clinic, organized an intra-hospital newspaper, *Notre Journal,* and established an open clinic in collaboration with psychiatrist Raymond Lacaton. Fanon, with the help of his assistant Jacques Azoulay and a nursing team, developed a cooperative framework described as an 'experimental milieu' involving 'bi-weekly ward meetings, as well as staff meetings, newspaper meetings, and bi-monthly celebrations'.[17] A key component of these therapeutic endeavours was the 'Film Committee', which adopted a unique approach to film image which was also then discussed in *Notre Journal.*

---

17   Frantz Fanon and Jacques Azoulay, 'Social Therapy in a Ward of Muslim Men: Methodological Difficulties', in Fanon, *Alienation and Freedom,* pp. 353–71 (p. 354).

In 1953, Fanon was facing extreme difficulties at Blida-Joinville, which were caused by the racist ethnopsychiatry of the Algiers School on the one hand, and the bloodshed of the anti-colonial war on the other. In that very same year, Oury initiated a series of institutional experiments attempting a disalienation and decolonization of the psychiatric care practice in the frame of La Borde clinic in Cour-Cheverny, France. From the very beginning, he was accompanied in this new experiment by Félix Guattari in particular:

> By 1953, Félix was already very active in the collective invention of La Borde, and came there from time to time. It was in August 1955 that Oury asked him to join and truly settle and work there. It was the time of organizing all the functional infrastructure of the place.[18]

At La Borde, Guattari was responsible for the implementation of extra-medical activities, including in particular the organizational structure of the 'grid', which implied a rotational work schedule of tasks and activities. Those shifting positions were meant to prevent the calcification of roles that led to institution's mental and social alienation. This 'internal mini-revolution' required 'all service personnel work to be integrated with medical work, and that, reciprocally, medical staff be drafted for material tasks such as cleaning, cooking, dishwashing, maintenance'.[19] 'I came to La Borde as an activist', Guattari states in a conversation

---

18   Clara Novaes and Ana Carolina Patto, 'Félix et Jean. Des terrains vagues de la Garenne-Colombes à l'expérience de La Borde', *Chimères*, 102 (2023), pp. 129–42 (p. 136).

19   Félix Guattari, 'La Borde: A Clinic Unlike Any Other', in *Chaosophy: Texts and Interviews 1972–1977*, ed. by Sylvère Lotringer, and trans. by David L. Sweet, Jarred Becker, and Taylor Adkins (Los Angeles: Semiotext(e), 2009), pp. 176–94 (p. 178). See also, for instance, the prolific work on this topic by Susana Caló, including 'The Grid', in

with psychiatrist and psychoanalyst Danielle Sivadon. 'I started organizing workshops, meetings, schedules, much like how I had organized the political cells I was involved in.'[20]

Guattari's relation to Saint-Alban was not only mediated by Oury. Indeed, he spent a month as a patient at the Lozerien hospital in 1956. According to him, thanks to this time there, he became aware of the importance of leaving more space for the patients, 'letting them alone for a bit'. The Saint-Alban experience had a crucial impact on Guattari's institutional practice, described as a 'mutation' and 'decentring of the subjectivity' in an institutional context.[21]

The text by Oury presented in this volume engages with the role he played in the legacy of institutional psychotherapy, and in particular with the foundation of La Borde. However, it is important to note that, except for Tosquelles, Oury does not mention other people in this text, and there is an omission of the names of female psychiatrists, caregivers, and psychoanalysts. In this sense, we feel it is crucial to acknowledge how the La Borde experiment was in fact

---

Anthropocene Curriculum, 23 April 2016 <https://www.anthropocene-curriculum.org/contribution/the-grid> [accessed 7 April 2024].

20   Félix Guattari and Danielle Sivadon, 'Le Préjugé démocratique. Juin 1987', *Chimères*, 94 (2019), pp. 144–48 (p. 146). This conversation was filmed by François Pain in May 1986, 'Le Divan de Félix', chaosmosemedia, 2021 <https://chaosmosemedia.net/2021/05/25/le-divan-de-felix/> [accessed 7 April 2024].

21   In Guattari's own words: 'Tosquelles's great strength was his consistent stance as a political activist. Let's be clear, this doesn't mean he was conveying political ideas, but rather that his manner of being, in any situation, was political. This is something hard to articulate, and perhaps I'm particularly attuned to it through some form of unspoken complicity with him. At Saint-Alban, Tosquelles immediately adopted this approach, whether interacting with the nuns, staff members, or the supervisory administrative entities. He operated with a militant logic that was more an existential logic than merely a matter of ideological content' (Guattari and Sivadon, 'Le Préjugé démocratique', p. 147).

a radically collective endeavour. Its constant reinvention throughout the years was only possible thanks to the participation and intervention of figures such as Micheline Kao, Gisela Pankow, Anne Querrien, Danielle Sivadon, Ginette Michaud, Jean-Claude Polack, François Pain, and Fernand Deligny. Indeed, this collective activity is reflected in the journal *Recherches*, edited by Centre d'études, de recherche et de formation institutionnelles (CERFI), and groups closely associated with it.[22]

Even though each new site modelled upon institutional psychotherapy developed its own specific strategies — as for instance the patient-run 'Hospital Committee', mentioned in Oury's text, or the Club, which functioned differently, according to the singular conditions of each institution — the experience of Saint-Alban was foundational for those transformations and deterritorializations. It laid the ground for sector psychiatry, schizoanalysis, and for other disalienist approaches situated closer to anti-psychiatry and its programme of deinstitutionalization.

TOWARDS A MATERIALIST AND RELATIONAL PSYCHIATRY

Both texts included in this volume deal with a certain conception of psychiatry. On the one hand, they criticize a purely mechano- and organo-oriented practice of care — one that would correlate mental disorders only with a disturbance localized in the patient's body. On the other hand,

---

22   Centre for Institutional Study, Research, and Development (CERFI) was a transdisciplinary research cooperative formed of psychiatrists, sociologists, video artists, educators, urbanists, architects, and economists. See Susana Caló's and Godofredo Pereira's project on this topic: 'CERFI: Militant Analysis, Collective Equipment and Institutional Programming', *Royal Collect of Art* <https://www.rca.ac.uk/research-innovation/projects/cerfi-militant-analysis-collective-equipment-and-institutional-programming/> [accessed 7 April 2024].

Fig. 10. The yearly 'Fête votive' (patronal feast) celebration at Saint-Alban, which is dedicated to the region's saint, invites the inhabitants of Lozère to dance, play games, and dress up in masks and costumes. Film still from Hélène Álvarez Tosquelles and François Tosquelles, *Société lozérienne d'hygiène mentale* (Lozerien Society of Mental Hygiene), Institut Jean Vigo — Cinémathèque de Perpignan, 1954–57. Courtesy Michel Tosquelles.

FIG. 11. The yearly 'Fête votive' (patronal feast) celebration
at Saint-Alban, which is dedicated to the region's saint,
invites the inhabitants of Lozère to dance, play games, and
dress up in masks and costumes. Film still from Hélène
Álvarez Tosquelles and François Tosquelles, *Société
lozérienne d'hygiène mentale* (Lozerien Society of Mental
Hygiene), Institut Jean Vigo — Cinémathèque de Perpignan,
1954–57. Courtesy Michel Tosquelles.

they propose an understanding of mental disorders according to a more complex vision, that is, implying that they necessarily maintain a relation to several elements such as the subject's social and perceptual milieu and its alteration, their particular history, and their conflicts. According to this vision, psychic suffering is marked by a problem in the world of a subject's relations and the only way to treat it is to reconstruct (or to construct new) relations.

Oury's 'Institutional Psychotherapy: From Saint-Alban to La Borde', was written only two years after the events of May 1968, a period marked by both a new critical energy and a severe conservative counter-reaction, which aimed at the 'recuperation' of the meaning of such events and at the subversion of their possible revolutionary consequences.[23] As Oury remarks, during the war years, psychiatry, ethics, and politics had become intrinsically connected. He has here in mind, of course, the Saint-Alban experience and the connection between psychiatry and resistance. However, writing almost three decades later, these years had started to recede from people's memories. Oury's text is marked by a certain urgency to recall this history, insisting that the eagerness for reinvention that marked those years continually needs to be reactualized. Furthermore, his lecture is historically situated in the wake of a new era for psychiatry following the introduction of antipsychotics in early 1970s — their popularization would happen over the span of the 1980s — and the harsh critique of psychoanalysis. For these reasons, Oury deemed it necessary to recall the history of institutional psychotherapy, retracing its trajectory from Lozère to Cour-Cheverny.

---

23   See Serge Audier, *La Pensée anti-68. Essai sur les origines d'une restauration intellectuelle* (Paris: La Découverte, 2008).

Oury highlights many of the practical principles developed by institutional psychotherapy: the fight against segregation and 'concentrationary' forms that psychiatry usually tends to develop; the importance of 'break[ing] down hierarchical barriers'; the creation of spaces inside the hospital that follow an 'axiom' of the 'freedom of circulation', that is, that patients should be able to freely move around inside its spaces — a hospital should not be conceived as a prison — ; the instituting of a self-governed society inside the hospital ('a society which will manage itself'); the transversality of psychic care and its connection to other social and pedagogical movements.

Oury notes that many of the principles practised at La Borde go back to strategic inventions by Tosquelles that could help disarticulate institutional rigidity imposed by the traditional top-down organization of establishments. He mentions in particular the creation of a sub-structure inside the institution: the hospital committee or the Croix-Marine society. This peculiar status given to such instances was used as a strategy so that different patients' organizations (such as the Club, for example) could exist autonomously and beyond the control of the hospital administration. In this way, what would eventually be produced by patients inside the hospital — in ergotherapy sessions or in the cafés, for example — and subsequently sold by them could also be reverted to these intra-institutional organizations and managed by them accordingly. Furthermore, this status could help prevent the administration from exploiting the patient workforce for the hospital's own interest — for example, to improve facilities or to generate money for the administration. As such, the patients could have a budget of their own to realize their preferred activities (a diner, a party, a painting atelier, a game, etc.), or in other words, to facilitate a cultural and social life inside the

FIG. 12. The yearly 'Fête votive' (patronal feast) celebration at Saint-Alban, which is dedicated to the region's saint, invites the inhabitants of Lozère to dance, play games, and dress up in masks and costumes. Film still from Hélène Álvarez Tosquelles and François Tosquelles, *Société lozérienne d'hygiène mentale* (Lozerien Society of Mental Hygiene), Institut Jean Vigo — Cinémathèque de Perpignan, 1954–57. Courtesy Michel Tosquelles.

FIG. 13. The yearly 'Fête votive' (patronal feast) celebration at Saint-Alban, which is dedicated to the region's saint, invites the inhabitants of Lozère to dance, play games, and dress up in masks and costumes. Film still from Hélène Álvarez Tosquelles and François Tosquelles, *Société lozérienne d'hygiène mentale* (Lozerien Society of Mental Hygiene), Institut Jean Vigo — Cinémathèque de Perpignan, 1954–57. Courtesy Michel Tosquelles.

psychiatric hospital that is adapted solely to the patients' needs and interests. The Club and other intra-institutional entities allow for the patients to leave the stasis of the hospitalized life and to once again take an active part in organizing their own group and social life. It works as a sort of *dispositif* (apparatus) of conviviality, relationality, and of culture, producing an exchange between patients, but also between them and non-patients. Such a strategy is a perfect example of how the autonomy given to the Club, for example, was also a form of resistance to the re-production of capitalist functioning and the exploitation of labour, which traditional hospitals replicated when putting patients to work, thus transforming them simply into workers of a company.[24]

Tosquelles's 'Psychotherapy and Dialectical Material-ism', constitutes the core of this volume. It is a dense theoretical text, in which the author develops a reflection on the scientific and philosophical status of the psychiatric discipline. It was written and presented in the aftermath of World War II, at a time when the transitional government had been established after the Liberation (1945–48), when Charles de Gaulle and the French Communist Party were still negotiating state repartitions, as well as new political and institutional programmes. Psychiatry was, at that moment, a discipline without any institutional and epistemo-logical autonomy, since it was subordinated to neurology — this had been the case since the psychiatry law of 1838

---

24 It is precisely as Ginette Michaud remarks in the following passage: 'We can see that the [traditional] hospital's economic structure is a replica of a capitalist company in our society, an alienating society to which we owe the numerous cases of "social maladjustment", those very people who are locked up in hospitals, whose jurisdiction clearly transcribes the relations of alienation.' See Ginette Michaud, *Laborde... un pari nécessaire. De la notion d'institution à la psychothérapie institutionnelle* (Paris: Gauthier-Villars/Bordas, 1977), p. 58.

and would only change after 1968 with a new decree.[25] Also for these reasons, psychiatry had a very unstable and debatable status — a discipline 'in crisis', as Sophie Lesage notes in her contextualizing and introductory 'Note to the Reader'.

Tosquelles's navigation of Marxism and psychiatry can be viewed as dialectical intervention — an articulation of a double critique. On the one side, he appeals to dialectical materialism in order to critically reveal the stasis of nosological categories; on the other — which is perhaps less obvious — one finds the repercussions of this dynamic understanding of psychiatry on his reading of dialectical materialism. 'Society, the nervous system, and the organism in general are not irreducible, isolated compartments', Tosquelles states.[26] As a result, the work of psychiatric disalienation needs to be considered as 'a "disalienation of the total fact of madness": the sick person, the asylum, *and* the psychiatrist at once'.[27] Already in 1945, institutional psychotherapy regarded 'madness' as a 'disorder in the relationship between the self and the world'.[28] Combining Marxist analysis with *Gestalt* psychology, alienation was conceptualized as a double estrangement: both mental and social alienation of the self from its 'participation in the

---

25 Henri Ey played an important role in these debates, defending an autonomy for psychiatry and criticizing the hospital-centrism of the old institutional mode of functioning. For further details on the discussion see Robert Castel, *La Gestion des risques* (Paris: Les Éditions de Minuit, 2011). The general *prise de parole* of 1968 certainly influenced this debate and was praised by Ey. A famous poster produced during the demonstrations of this period even claimed: 'dénonçons la psychiatrie policière' ('Let us denounce police-related psychiatry').

26 Tosquelles, 'Psychopathology and Dialectical Materialism', p. 65.

27 Ibid., p. 72.

28 Lucien Bonnafé and others, 'Valeur de la théorie de la forme en psychiatrie: la dialectique du moi et du monde et l'événement morbide', *Annales médico-psychologiques*, 103.2 (1945), pp. 279–84 (p. 280).

environment'.[29] Such a holistic view undoes any progressivist ideology in favour of an ethical stance, an 'activation' extending even to the reader, as Sophie Lesage describes in her text.[30] Similarly, according to Tosquelles, the subject's emotional manifestations reveal a dialectics of 'action and reaction' — emotion seen as agency and the potential for action and not merely as a reaction — in such a way that undoes the linear and teleological relation between cause and effect.

This Marxist perspective allows Tosquelles to question the classical division between history and nature, theory and practice, as he sees 'every "action" or "situation"' bearing witness to 'the human being's active presence in the world'. Thus, 'history' itself appears as 'social physiology': 'There is no thought without a human brain, no human brain outside of the person [*hors de l'homme*], nor person outside of the world'.[31]

Many of the problems Tosquelles was confronted with at the end of the 1940s were related to a solely organo-oriented perspective of psychiatry. Against this reductionist view, Tosquelles advanced the phenomenological and existential dimension of the individual's lived experience developed in his contemporaneous doctoral dissertation, defended in 1948 and later published under the title *Le Vécu de la fin du monde dans la folie. Le Témoignage de Gérard de Nerval* (The Lived Experience of the End of the World in Madness: The Testimony of Gérard de Nerval). In this work, the psychiatrist took up the challenge of thinking the experience of catastrophe in at least three dimensions: in its clinical manifestation, expressed through the form of

---

29 Ibid.

30 Sophie Lesage, 'Note to the Reader on 'Psychopathology and Dialectical Materialism', in this volume, p. 46.

31 Tosquelles, 'Psychopathology and Dialectical Materialism', p. 59.

schizophrenia; in its political and historical scope, in the inscription of the war; and in its atmospheric and poetic manifestation, through a concerted analysis of Gérard de Nerval's novel *Aurélia*, written shortly before the poet's suicide. Tosquelles introduced the German notion of *Erlebnis* (lived experience) from phenomenology and existential philosophy to conceptualize the relation between the singularity of an experience and the world it engenders. 'What is at stake', Tosquelles writes, 'is the dynamic which produces the lived experience [*experience vécu*] of a person giving it its existential efficacy'.[32] *Erlebnis* etymologically inscribes 'life' (in German *Leben*) into experience, highlighting for Tosquelles the irreducible dimension of the lived temporality of 'the end of the world', and at the same time its complex, paradoxical continuity.

From this perspective, Tosquelles criticizes the scientific isolation of the brain from the rest of the organism and its situatedness in an environment, the 'intra-organic correlations' from the external processes.[33] In 'Psychotherapy and Dialectical Materialism' he claims that psychiatry, as every other scientific discipline, blindly subscribes to philosophical — or ideological — presuppositions that must be critically analysed, placing these in a concrete historical situation of a lived experience. Dialectical materialism and Marxism would be the method *par excellence* for undertaking such a critique, since it does not fall into the trap or the 'error of taking *processes in isolation*'.[34] Tosquelles follows here materialist psychologist Henri Wallon in particular for whom dialectical materialism constitutes a science different from others because it does not immobilize things,

---

32   Tosquelles, *Le Vécu de la fin du monde dans la folie*, p. 51.
33   Tosquelles, 'Psychopathology and Dialectical Materialism', p. 55.
34   Ibid., p. 54.

but instead tries to understand them in their permanent state of movement in relation to other things, and in their continual and processual becoming.

For Tosquelles, dialectical materialism appears even more urgent with regard to psychiatry than to other disciplines because of the specificity of its object: the human individual. Psychiatry's object, to a greater extent in comparison to other disciplines, could not be taken abstractly, isolated and separated from its concrete situation, its milieu, its history, and its development; in sum, its object constitutes an extremely complex and mutable one. Tosquelles accepts the usual definition of psychiatry as a science dealing with an 'anomaly of thought, belief, and action'.[35] But, in order to deal with its problem, psychiatry would need to embrace situatedness, complexity, and relationality while considering the individual in its complex somatic, temporal, and psychic relations to the environment. Medicine emerges not as a nosological pursuit of abstractions, but a materialist and *situated practice* of concrete constellations, each time necessitating its own reinvention.

Indeed, Tosquelles goes back to a conception of psychiatry founded on relationality — patient-doctor relation crucially taken in a complex clinical environment — and on experimentation rather than on nosography and, as a result, a mythology of the 'organism' or, in his words, a 'mythology of brain localizations'.[36] According to him, psychiatry should be based on 'trial and error', on the 'purest empiricism' in which 'techniques and therapeutics follow one another and, along the way, present us with new problems. It is in trying to solve these problems that new techniques are discovered. In this way, a dialectic of

---

35   Ibid., p. 72.

36   Ibid., p. 69.

thought, experience, techniques, and object is established, in which each part conditions the whole, and the whole conditions each part'.[37]

Dialectical materialism can be seen as a tool, which helps to complexify the psychiatric fact by posing that madness never exists as such, as an isolable and neutral category: it is always correlated to its actual society and its history, and even the psychiatrist is not an external observer, but also appears in the equation, since they do not stand 'outside the world; they are integral to their epoch and subject to its technological and social influences'.[38] Tosquelles thus surely subscribes to a Marxist conception of the human being according to which the human always appears in socially conditioned and concrete situations. That is why, in this sense, the psychiatric field needs to relate also to a sociological one; only then is it able to produce more effective diagnoses and treatments. For this precise reason, he thinks that positions more oriented towards positivism, such as that defended by Auguste Comte, had denied the very possibility of the existence of psychology as science, a problem that was now posed to psychiatry as well.

Relating psychiatry to its social field does not mean, however, that there should be the pure social before the individual. Tosquelles argues that this other extreme would also constitute a non-dialectical position. Indeed, he is interested in what could be called the 'socio-genesis' of the individual — an idea that he finds in Jacques Lacan's doctoral dissertation,[39] which resonates with Georges Politzer's con-

---

37   Ibid., p. 71.

38   Ibid., p. 66.

39   Jacques Lacan, *De la psychose paranoïaque dans ses rapports avec la personnalité* [1932] (Paris: Seuil, 1975).

crete psychology,[40] and will also find echoes in Fanon's *sociogenesis*.[41]

Tosquelles — and later Oury — aligns with a current that he names 'non-conformist psychiatrists', including names such as Georges Daumézon, Pankow, Bonnafé, and others who opposed themselves to the school of Georges Heuyer. As professor to a whole generation from Lacan to Daumézon himself, Heuyer defended a very organo-oriented position and compared the fight against mental illness to the fight against tuberculosis: prevention, treatment, aftercare, and isolation. On the one hand, his position identified mental health and socius, but on the other, it naturalized such a relation and imposed the need for immediate isolation and treatment focused on the sick individual. Madness, following this line, was an illness to be treated as a pure clinical object.

Tosquelles certainly follows the principle of 'biological unity of the organism and its milieu'.[42] But the fundamental notion of 'milieu' is here to be understood also as a complex one, implying the historical, social, cultural, and biological situation in which an individual evolves.[43] Wal-

---

40   Georges Politzer, 'La Fin de la psychanalyse' [1939], in *Écrits 2. Les Fondements de la psychologie* (Paris: Éditions sociales, 1973), available online at <https://wikilivres.org/wiki/La_fin_de_la_psychanalyse> [accessed 7 April 2024].

41   Frantz Fanon, *Black Skin, White Masks*, trans. by Charles Lam Markmann (London: Pluto Press, 1986), p. 13.

42   Tosquelles, 'Psychopathology and Dialectical Materialism', p. 55. A statement that will find echoes in those by 'red' psychiatrists Louis Le Guillant and Lucien Bonnafé: 'Thus, the indissoluble unity of the individual and the milieu, which is of course a historical unity, a dialectical one, is the fundamental law, the law from which the normal or ill psyche, the patient in toto is unable to escape' (Le Guillant, 'Introduction à une psychopathologie sociale', *L'Évolution psychiatrique*, 19.1 (1954), pp. 1–52 (p. 19)).

43   Among other theoretical sources that were determinant to Tosquelles's thinking on the milieu — and later to Oury and Fanon as well — were

lon is indeed the key-figure in this debate. He had defined the object of psychology not as being the individual's interiority, but 'a situation'.[44] Also, in opposition to Jean Piaget, he considered the individual, since their preverbal stages, as totally immersed in the milieu.

The non-conformist psychiatrists engaged in clinical practice in the opposite direction of that proposed by Heuyer and his students. Not isolation, but resocialization; not passive, one-directional, and localized treatment, but a holistic approach based on the activation of the patient through social practices. The institutional project here was indeed 'the conversion of the asylum into a social milieu'.[45]

It is surely a question of non-conformism. It could also be called a disalienist tendency, which would get different more or less radical variations according to the positions developed over time by Tosquelles, Fanon, or Oury, to cite only these three. This non-conformist, disalienist, resistant tone seems to be absent in the discursive fields today dealing with care, clinical work, psychiatry. Against this backdrop, institutional psychotherapy's ethically engaged and

---

Kurt Goldstein and Georges Canguilhem. Both of them introduced a 'normative' and 'adaptive' milieu-based theory. In *Der Aufbau des Organismus*, the first posited that an organism maintains equilibrium with its surroundings through a sequence of 'catastrophic reactions' (Kurt Goldstein, *The Organism: A Holistic Approach to Biology Derived from Pathological Data in Man* (New York: Zone Books, 1995), p. 392). This perspective was further developed by Canguilhem, who emphasized the organism's potential to set its own norms. See Georges Canguilhem, *The Normal and the Pathological* (New York: Zone Books, 1991). Building on such ideas, Tosquelles sees schizophrenia not as a mere loss of the world but as a creative effort: an attempt at reconstruction of the shattered world. Therefore, Tosquelles views madness not as a state of passivity but as a manifestation of prolific energy, marked by 'freedom' and a sense of 'responsibility'. See Tosquelles, *Le Vécu de la fin du monde dans la folie*, p. 98.

44 Henri Wallon, *De l'acte à la pensée* (Paris: Flammarion, 1942), p. 50.

45 Tosquelles, 'Psychopathology and Dialectical Materialism', p. 73.

politicized practice — whose texts were barely translated into English until now — only gains its current topicality and urgency, in particular in times of super-abundance of diagnoses and increased psychic suffering rates.[46] The pharmacology-based ideology that dominates medical institutions and the unsuccessful attempts, first of genetics, and then of neuroscience, of giving a 'definitive' answer to the problem of *madness,* show that there is still a lot to learn from the clinical-political struggles of the twentieth century. This 'problem' cannot be dissociated from human agency and the world in which it takes place. In this sense, it will remain associated with ongoing struggles for transforming the social conditions of hospitalization and medicalization, as well as the institutional and societal issues of segregation.

---

46   Very recently, three publications related to Tosquelles appeared in English: *Francesc Tosquelles: Avant-Garde Psychiatry, Radical Politics, and Art,* ed. by Carles Guerra, Joana Masó, Valérie Rousseau, and Edward Dioguardi (New York: American Folk Art Museum, 2024); Francesc Tosquelles, 'A Politics of Madness', trans. by Perwana Nasif, *Parapraxis,* 4 (August 2024); and Joana Masó, 'The Collective's Women', trans. by Perwana Nazif and Jesse Newberg, *Parapraxis,* 4 (August 2024).

Note to the Reader on 'Psychopathology and Dialectical Materialism'

SOPHIE LESAGE

An unsigned introductory note (revised by François Tosquelles) accompanies the typescript of this talk, titled 'Psychopathology in Light of Dialectical Materialism':

> This text has never been published.
>
> It is the second lecture in a series on 'Methods in Knowledge of the Human in Neurology and Psychiatry Today' organized at and by the École

---

*   Editors' and translator's note: Sophie Lesage (née Legrain) is the founder and principal editor of Éditions d'une, an independent publishing platform that emerged in 2014 from the work on the publication of the GTPSI proceedings (Groupe de travail de psychothérapie et de sociothérapie institutionnelles — which in English translates as Working Group for Institutional Psychotherapy and Sociotherapy). She is the editor of the original French publication of 'Psychopathology and Dialectical Materialism'. This introduction accompanied the publication of Tosquelles's text.

normale supérieure in 1947. Of course, Minkowski, Lacan, Follin,[1] and others developed their perspectives on this occasion. The paradox that the organizers embraced involved suggesting the development of what one might call 'psychopathology in light of dialectical materialism' to someone who was not a member of the Communist Party — some of whose active members may have expressed views not always aligned with the stated ideology.

With the help of Tosquelles's accent, a lively debate between Zazzo and others divided various speakers, not without confusion, about the use of tests in 'scientific psychology'.[2] Without dismissing the value of statistical work, Tosquelles accentuated the value of the complex and concrete dynamics of the emerging event, linking the prejudices of the tester and the fears or hopes of the tested: 'The relationship is not symmetrical, as one might expect from certain imaginary or real twins, or from mirror effects, those of a double'; 'Wallon denounced this type of imaginary fascination, or what he calls the psychology of motor images (sic)'.[3]

---

1   Translator's note: Eugène Minkowski (1885–1972) was a French psychiatrist known for his work in phenomenological psychiatry and contributions to the understanding of schizophrenia, emphasizing patients' subjective experience, for example through his influential concept of 'lived time'. Sven Follin (1911–1997) was a French psychiatrist noted for his active involvement in the Communist resistance during World War II. He contributed significantly to the reform and humanization of psychiatric practices in France.

2   Translator's note: René Zazzo (1910–1995) was a French psychologist who contributed to developmental and child psychology. As a student of Henri Wallon, Zazzo brought a Marxist perspective to his research. He is noted for his studies on twins, which he conducted not only in the laboratory, but in real-life environments.

3   Translator's note: Henri Wallon (1879–1962) was a French Marxist psychologist noted for applying dialectical materialism to developmental and child psychology. His research focused on the interplay between the child's cognitive development and social, cultural, collective, and individual historical contexts.

> Regardless, this lecture — which they admitted to
> having 'misunderstood' — led to two incidental
> listeners deciding to leave Paris to work at Saint-
> Alban: these were Robert Millon and his friend
> Jean Oury.[4] It is therefore worth revisiting here,
> especially as Tosquelles has sometimes said, per-
> haps misleadingly in shorthand, that institutional
> psychotherapy has always walked on two legs:
> that of Freudian theory and that of Marxist theory.
> Here, Tosquelles articulates what he believes to
> be the Marxist dimension, quite far from what is
> often expected.

This is the second talk, dated 5 February 1947, in a series
of lectures organized by Georges Gusdorf and Georges
Daumézon on 'Methods in Knowledge of the Human in
Neurology and Psychiatry Today'.[5] It followed the third
Bonneval meeting (September 1946).[6]

---

4   Translator's note: Robert Millon (1923–2009) was a French psychiatrist associated with institutional psychotherapy and a close friend of
Jean Oury. He was an initial member of GTPSI. After working at Saint-
Alban (1947–49, as an intern at the same time as Oury; then 1952–55
as medical director), he practised in Grenoble, where he was involved
in the MFPF (French Movement for Family Planning).

5   Translator's note: Held as a prisoner of war by the Germans from 1940
to 1945, French philosopher Georges Gusdorf (1912–2000) worked
as head tutor (*caïman*) at the École normale supérieure after the war
ended. Interested in psychology and psychopathology, he wanted to
introduce his students (among them Louis Althusser and Michel Foucault) to psychiatry. With the help of his friend, French psychiatrist
Georges Daumézon, Gusdorf organized not only the 1947 lecture
series, but also visitations of patients at Sainte-Anne hospital and an-
nual excursions to the psychiatric hospital of Fleury-les-Aubrais in
the Loiret department. Under the auspices of Daumézon as medical
director, many activities and methods associated with institutional psychotherapy had been implemented in this hospital. See Didier Eribon,
Michel Foucault, trans. by Betsy Wing (Cambridge, MA: Harvard University Press, 1991), p. 41.

6   The proceedings of these meetings have been published: *Le Problème
de la psychogenèse des névroses et des psychoses*, ed. by Henri Ey (Paris:
Desclée de Brouwer, 1950; repr. Paris: Tchou, 2004). See also note
13 on p. 44. [Translator's note: *Journées de Bonneval* were a series of

Despite my efforts, I was unable to fully bring to light the content of these sessions, which are significant for the historiography of psychiatry in the immediate post-war period.[7] I have nevertheless put together a certain number of clues. In addition to the participants mentioned above, Jean Oury also details the participation in these lectures of [Julián de] Ajuriaguerra, [Pierre] Naville, and [Lucien] Bonnafé.[8] It can be assumed that Bonnafé's lecture was

---

conferences hosted by Henri Ey in Bonneval in the Eure-et-Loir department, where Ey was director of the psychiatric hospital from 1933 on. For the third of these meetings, titled 'Causalité psychique des troubles mentaux' (Psychic Causality of Mental Disorders) held in September 1946, he invited psychoanalysts and psychiatrists to discuss the topic of psychogenesis. The participants seized this occasion to challenge Ey's position, known as 'organo-dynamism'. In particular, Lacan criticized Ey's doctrine as being organicist 'because it cannot relate the genesis of mental problems as such [...] to anything but the play of systems constituted in the material substance [*l'étendue*] located within the body's integument' (Jacques Lacan, *Écrits: The First Complete Edition in English*, trans. by Bruce Fink in collaboration with Héloïse Fink and Russell Grigg (New York: W. W. Norton, 2006), p. 124). Tosquelles recalls preparing the 1946 Bonneval conference and Oury mentions him attending it (*Recherches*, 17 (1975), p. 109). The published proceedings of these meetings include a contribution by Sven Follin and Lucien Bonnafé that Tosquelles refers to (see Tosquelles, 'Psychopathology and Dialectical Materialism', p. 66). Thus, the lecture series at the École normale supérieur and Tosquelles's talk can be seen as a continuation of the third Bonneval conference.]

7   Archives may still exist at the École normale supérieure at Rue d'Ulm.

8   See Jean Oury, *L'Aliénation* (Paris: Galilée, 1992), pp. 20–21. [Translator's note: Julián de Ajuriaguerra (1911–1993) was a Basque-French neuropsychiatrist and neurologist who would later become professor at Collège de France. He was an active member of the Batia group (see also note 13 on p. 44). Pierre Naville (1904–1993) was a French sociologist, writer, and politician. A prominent figure in the French Surrealist movement during its early stage, he later became known for his work in the sociology of work and his contributions to Marxist theory. Lucien Bonnafé (1912–2003) was a French psychiatrist who played a key role in the early development of institutional psychotherapy during the Occupation and in the sectorization of psychiatry in France. Bonnafé stayed at Saint-Alban from 1942 to 1946 and it was due to him that figures like Paul Éluard and Georges Canguilhem found a temporary hiding place in the isolated hospital in the Lozère department.]

revised and published at the end of the following year.[9] In his own talk, Tosquelles also mentions having heard [Sven] Follin describe the drama of the 'domestic torturers' a few days earlier, thereby revisiting an earlier work with [Jean] Dublineau.[10] And it might be his own contribution that [Jacques] Lacan refers to in a letter of 1963: 'Our ties are old, Althusser. You surely remember that lecture I gave at Normale [École normale supérieure] after the war, a crude rudiment for an obscure moment (yet one of the actors in my present drama found his path there)'[11] …

Obscure indeed is this moment in history and in psychiatry, which Tosquelles, echoing others ([Paul] Balvet, Daumézon, and [Henri] Ey in particular), describes as 'in crisis'.[12] In the subsequent debates on the relation-

---

9   Lucien Bonnafé, 'Interprétation du fait psychiatrique selon la méthode historique de K. Marx et F. Engels', *L'Évolution psychiatrique*, [13].4 (1948), pp. 75–105.

10 Jean Dublineau and Sven Follin, 'Examen clinique d'un "bourreau domestique". Rôle des interactions conjugales', *Annales médico-psychologiques*, 100.1 (1942), pp. 326–29. [Translator's note: Jean Dublineau (1900–1975) was a French physician and psychiatrist with a focus on child psychiatry. During his training he came into close contact with Georges Heuyer. Dublineau initiated Sven Follin and Lucien Bonnafé in child psychiatry.]

11 Letter reproduced in *Magazine littéraire*, 304 (1992), p. 49. It is known that a lecture given by Lacan at the Ecole normale supérieure at Rue d'Ulm was decisive for Jean Oury, who remained in contact with Lacan until the latter's death.

12 At the same time that Tosquelles was speaking, Paul Balvet wrote: 'Psychiatrists are criticized for their lack of initiative and their isolation: in turn, they challenge outdated legislation, antiquated facilities, and routine administration. The lack of serenity of some of these explanations, their aggressiveness, already makes them suspect […]. It seems that a collective guilty conscience seeks to justify itself among some and others; either by hiding the miserable situation of the alienated person, or by proving that one has done what one could and that it did not depend on oneself that things would turn out this way' ('De l'autonomie de la profession psychiatrique', in *Au-delà de l'asile d'aliénés et de l'hôpital psychiatrique*, Documents de *L'Information psychiatrique* (Paris: Desclée de Brouwer, 1946), pp. 11–18). For other analyses, see

ship between neurology and psychiatry,[13] the questioning of Marxism and psychology mobilizes both philosophers and psychiatrists; Tosquelles focuses on the nature and meaning that the confrontation between dialectical materialism and psychopathology can have, thereby linking social alienation and mental alienation from the field of *culture*: 'Dialectical materialism has to be posited on a cultural level, which is not to say that this possibility is unrelated to the "battle of nations and classes".[14]

To situate these works 'in their development'[15] may indeed require a work of cultivation; upholding the con-

---

also Tosquelles, 'Psychopathology and Dialectical Materialism', p. 67, n. 38.

13 Note the existence at this time of the Batia group (led by Julián de Ajuriaguerra in particular), which initiated the publication of the debate at the *Journées de Bonneval* in 1943; see the preface of *Les Rapports de la neurologie et de la psychiatrie*, ed. by Henri Ey, Julián de Ajuriaguerra, and Henry Hécaen (Paris: Hermann, 1947), not included in the 1998 reprint. [Translator's note: Batia (or Batea, which is Basque for 'ensemble' (together) according to Bonnafé) was a working group of psychiatrists and psychoanalysts formed around the time of the Liberation of France in 1944–45, with meetings often taking place at the residence of Ajuriaguerra. Other prominent members included Lacan, Bonnafé, Tosquelles, Daumézon, Follin, Louis Le Guillant, Henri Duchêne, Henry Hécaen, Julien Rouart, and Serge Lebovici. Drawing inspiration from the Bourbaki group of mathematicians at École normale supérieure, according to Daumézon, the group mainly discussed theoretical questions. Parallel to this and with overlapping personnel, the newly founded Syndicat des médecins des hôpitaux psychiatriques tackled the initiation of practical reforms in psychiatric hospitals. In addition to the publication of the proceedings of the second *Journées de Bonneval* held in 1943, the group prepared the 1946 *Journées de Bonneval* (see note 6 on pp. 41–42). In 1947, the Communist Party's condemnation of psychoanalysis exacerbated already existing internal conflicts, eventually leading to the dissolution of the group. For more detailed information on the Batia group see the testimonies of some of the participants in *Recherches*, 17 (1975), esp. pp. 107–10; 116–18; 551.]

14 Tosquelles, 'Psychopathology and Dialectical Materialism', p. 51.

15 See the section on 'Dialectical Materialism According to its Development', ibid., pp. 52–57.

tinuity of dialectical materialism with the experimental science conceptualized by Claude Bernard, Tosquelles rejects any *a priori* systematizing of the psychiatric *praxis* in order to better discern its 'object',[16] which is mobile by nature. It would therefore be inappropriate to see the following as merely a textual commentary aimed at applying Marxist knowledge to psychiatry.[17]

Quite the contrary, this text, at the cutting edge of the critical method embodied by Marx's *Economic and Philosophic Manuscripts of 1844*, proves inexhaustible in the usual explanatory mode — to the point of subverting it.[18] It certainly offers a set of very interesting references and ideas to be thematized. But the feat of this talk can only be grasped in its 'baroque' dressing in the Tosquellian sense — the dexterity of the discourse aiming to draw attention to these very formations. From 'gesture' to 'gestation', the active therapy advocated by Tosquelles relies, through metaphor and metonymy, on an aesthetic work [*travail esthétique*] in the primary sense of the term: an active reading.

> In their work, human beings invent — at the
> mercy of the winds — the sails of their ship.

---

16   See ibid., pp. 65–66.

17   See ibid., pp. 84–85. On the other hand, it can be seen as a continuation of the Politzerian endeavour; see ibid., pp. 74–75, n. 48 and Olivier Apprill, 'Tosquelles et la psychiatrie concrète', in *François Tosquelles et le travail*, ed. by Pascale Molinier (Paris: Éditions d'une, 2018), pp. 159–80.

18   The preparation of this text also led me to question the way in which the 1844 *Manuscripts* had been edited and then translated: this resulted in the translation (and forthcoming publication at Éditions d'une) of Margaret Fay's research writings on this question [Translator's note: 'The 1844 Economic and Philosophic Manuscripts of Karl Marx: A Critical Commentary and Interpretation' (unpublished doctoral thesis, University of California, Berkeley, 1979)], which have been little known in France until now, and therefore not taken into account in the editions and commentaries.

> They transfer values there and trade them in every port where they anchor: the interplay of metaphors and metonymies articulates the impossible reproduction of gesture and gestation with other humans… Through this, however, the articulatory chain of the verb in action binds them.[19]

His talk aims to convey not abstract representations, but an *activation* of the same kind as he contracted on the occasion of his own encounter with Marx's works — his 'POUMist'[20] views only partially aligned with the intellectual context of his audience. What will it be like today?

In its form, this text is unparalleled in the subsequent works of Tosquelles. Seventy years on, this first edition will allow us to appreciate its content in all its freshness — and even its relevance.

> We don't say that our actings [*agirs*] follow us, while we do say: our acts [*actes*] follow us. This is very important, and once again it raises the problem of repetition, of memory, and so on. The acting may follow us or may not, whereas our acts follow us, that's absolutely certain.[21]

TRANSLATED BY CHRISTIAN SCHEERHORN

---

19   François Tosquelles, *Psychiatrie, psychanalyse et politique* (Paris: Éditions d'une, forthcoming).

20   On this subject, see *Francesc Tosquelles. Psychiatre, catalan, marxiste*, ed. by Jacques Tosquellas (Paris: Éditions d'une, 2019). [Translator's note: POUM refers to Partit Obrer d'Unificació Marxista (The Workers' Party of Marxist Unification), an anti-Stalinist communist movement. It was established in 1935 through the merger of the Bloc Obrer i Camperol (BOC: Workers and Peasants' Bloc) and the Izquierda Comunista de España (ICE: Communist Left of Spain), with Tosquelles being one of its founding members.]

21   Remark by François Tosquelles on 31 January 1968 as part of Jacques Lacan's seminar on 'The Psychoanalytic Act'.

Psychopathology and Dialectical Materialism

FRANÇOIS TOSQUELLES

INTRODUCTION

Philosophy Has to Call Everything into Question, and So Does Science[1]

Ladies and Gentlemen,

If I have understood correctly the task I've been given in this cycle of lectures, it is a question, on the one hand,

---

*   Editors' note: According to the French editor, an alternative title was also mentioned in Tosquelles's typescript: *Psychopathology in Light of Dialectical Materialism*. The talk was part of a lecture series titled *Les Méthodes de connaissance de l'homme dans la neurologie et la psychiatrie actuelle* (Methods in Knowledge of the Human in Neurology and Psychiatry Today) held at the École normale supérieure in 1947. The title we have used here corresponds to the first French edition: François Tosquelles, *Psychopathologie et matérialisme dialectique* (Paris: Éditions d'une, 2019).

1   Translator's note: All headings and notes — unless otherwise indicated — are by the French editor, Sophie Lesage (née Legrain). Often these notes have been revised, thanks in particular to the attentive referencing work of Christian Scheerhorn.

of teasing out the conception of the human being [*de l'homme*][2] that emerges in applications of dialectical materialism to psychopathology and, on the other, of tracing the limits of this methodology. The programme seems clear. However, I foresee difficulties that derive, firstly, from the very posing of this problem: dialectical materialism would thus seem to be understood as *a philosophy,* the immutable principles of which are to be applied somewhere.[3]

Yet, a comparative study of Marxist texts has enabled me to understand that, while dialectical materialism claims to put an end to all philosophy *a priori*, it is *identified with the development of science* and apt to integrate any new conquest of the latter.[4] Admittedly, among anti-Marxists, or

---

2   Translator's note: The French word *l'homme* — much as the English 'man' once did — stands both for the male species and for humankind in general. In this text, Tosquelles employs the term almost exclusively in the latter sense. However, as customary English usage has shifted to what is considered more gender-neutral language, I have preferred to translate this French word with a range of other English words, such as person, human being, the human, humankind, depending on the context. This strategy became a little difficult, notably from a stylistic point of view, in the sections on Karl Marx. Marx uses the German word *Mensch*, which designates a human individual without the distinction of sex and has been conventionally rendered by the English term 'man'. For the aforementioned reason, the term has also been rendered using more gender-neutral language but this time at the risk of some awkwardness.

3   All italics have been carried over from the typescript.

4   Henri Wallon writes, notably: 'This dialectical materialism seeks to replace other theories of knowledge, because in their efforts to define things, they have immobilized them, because they have substituted their rigid frameworks for changing being, and because all too often they have taken themselves for being itself, whose existence they have reduced to that of the systems built to know it. Dialectical materialism, then, is not simply a theory of knowledge. It is undoubtedly the only one capable of translating the movement of ideas, the evolution of human knowledge and of the sciences, but also, by the same token, it is exactly in keeping with the very existence of things, which is becoming and movement.' See Henri Wallon, 'Matérialisme dialectique et psychologie', in *Les Cours de l'université nouvelle. Cours de philosophie* (Paris: Éditions sociales, 1946), pp. 15–23 (p. 15).

even, at times, among certain so-called Marxists, things do not always appear this way… But whether or not dialectical materialism has succeeded in its aim, [whether we actually manage] to define the essential features of its methodology, we're not well placed to delimit it.

If we admit that, as knowledge of the laws of development, dialectical materialism is *a posteriori* of science, how can we talk about its application to science?

To pose the problem from this logical perspective, it is true, would be to betray dialectical materialism: science is not a simple abstraction. Science, like any sector of reality, is a process of *becoming*, where the 'person of science/object' intersection can *be defined* as a two-way movement. This is why it is entirely legitimate to consider dialectical materialism both as posterior to science and as applicable to scientific research itself.

It is no less true that the general theme of this lecture series reveals a *philosophical intent* that may be the source of misunderstandings between us and our audience. Of course, this isn't the first time that persons trained in philosophy have approached medicine to ask for an introduction to 'human' problems. Nor is it the first time that doctors have risked appearing as philosophers. There is indeed a twofold movement that we can make coincide in evenings like this. Let's not be mistaken about the meaning and scope of this coincidence: the aim of philosopher-physicians is always rooted in the practice of the medical art; for them, excursions to the islands of philosophy are neither vacations nor passionate hobbies. As Claude Bernard has clearly shown, for philosopher-physicians philosophical developments are no more than an introduction to their practice. They are the ones who grasp the indispensable unity of theory and practice, of 'head and hand', as Claude Bernard used to say.[5] Science's failures are, for them, merely temporary. The physician cannot question science's value: *the power to know and to transform the sick person* ['l'homme malade'][6] *certainly remains to be conquered, but the existence of this power grounds the physician's concrete existence.*

Some believe that psychiatry is an exception to this rule. There are even psychiatrists who have come to psychiatry after having tasted philosophy, looking for solid ground from which to rise to the knowledge of the human. But there can be no doubt that if, owing

---

5   'To be worthy of this name, the experimenter must be at once a theoretician and a practitioner. If they are to possess in a full manner the art of instituting the facts of experience, which are the materials of science, they must also clearly be cognizant of the scientific principles that govern our reasoning amid the varied experimental study of natural phenomena. It would be impossible to separate these two things: the head and the hand. A skilful hand without the head that guides it is a blind instrument; the head without the hand that carries out remains impotent.' (Claude Bernard, *Introduction à l'étude de la médecine expérimentale* [1865] (Paris: Flammarion, 2008), p. 34).

6   Translator's note: Throughout the text, Tosquelles employs the word *malade* rather than *patient*. While *malade* is used in French in the same way that we would use 'patient' in English, and seemingly poses no problem — or little insofar as a patient is not necessarily ill — for the translator, there has also been a concerted effort by many in the French-speaking world to use *malade* instead of *patient* on grounds that we do not in English: whereas the latter denotes the individual taken into care by the medical apparatus, the one that passively receives the actions of the doctor, the former refers to the irreducibly socially active experience of the sick person, an aspect that Tosquelles is keen to underline in this talk. While there is a debate in English on what it means to be a 'patient' — connected to a global movement that demands patient rights — we do not have a separate word that would conveniently refer to this subjective dimension. So, in translating *le malade*, I have opted for a mix. I have translated phrases such as *l'homme malade* as 'sick person' where it made sense to retain the connection between sickness and social being at stake in Tosquelles's text, whereas when Tosquelles talks about the *médecin-malade* pairing, for instance, I have gone with 'patient', which sounds more natural to English ears and allows for economy of style.

to a *déformation professionelle*, such psychiatrists fail to overcome their origins and transform their aims, they will remain constrained to a contemplative sort of medicine — which is the negation of medicine as a social practice.

Philosophy has to call everything into question, and so does science. However, the philosopher's quest for knowledge has a different aim to the doctor's: to avoid seeing our coincidence as a source of misunderstanding, we ought to think through, in a frank and evident way, the two different planes on which we are going to elaborate our ideas.

And since we're laying all our cards on the table, I must confess my disquiet about elaborating on a topic that it seems difficult to place above the political conceptions one may have. As Pierre Naville put it recently, 'the problem of the scientific validity of dialectical materialism is essentially settled on the battlefields of nations and classes.'[7] A communist would, I believe, have the right to demand my place here for one of the Party's militant doctors... But we're not on a battlefield: I believe, together with the organizers of these talks, that the point is to remove the present investigation from any passionate attitude.

---

7 Revised note. These words are located in the 'Introduction' (dated 1 May 1945) of Naville's *Psychologie, marxisme, matérialisme* [1946] (Paris: Rivière, 1948), pp. 9–42. He adds: 'Nevertheless, nothing can prevent us from posing it also in its "cultural" terms, and generally speaking, the value of scientific and revolutionary thought has always been presented simultaneously under these two aspects. [...] The empiricism of political struggle, the purely pragmatic criterion of the success of an armed struggle is not enough, and will never be enough, to convince men of the absolute or even relative validity of a scientific conception, for the relations between them are of a particularly complex dialectic, where the structure of contradictions infinitely exceeds the crude forms of a synthetic triad. [...] It is in this sense that the question of the value and purpose of science can legitimately be raised in any age' (p. 10).

Dialectical materialism has to be posited on a cultural level, which is not to say that this possibility is unrelated to the 'battle of nations and classes': it's obvious that we wouldn't have had the opportunity to develop this conversation three years ago; on the other hand, there will be militants from various political sectors in the audience who, tying themselves to dialectical materialism, will have the opportunity to intervene at the end of my talk.

Dialectical Materialism According to its Development

I don't think we need to go into the basics of dialectical materialism. However, allow me to make an observation: in order to grasp any theory or conception of the world, it seems essential that we first make a leap of good faith, taking leave of ourselves to follow the original development of its internal logic. The point here is about grasping systems 'from within', even if it means that only afterwards can we see whether the 'results' agree or disagree with our body of knowledge, or can we analyse the justification for the foundation that underpins them.

As far as dialectical materialism is concerned, the approach is not going to be an easy one for us:

- first, because it is the *weapon of combat* of a social class;

- second, because we are not used to its *internal logical scaffolding*.

Yet, even with constant effort on our part, following the steps imposed by this method on our thinking will present pitfalls.

If you've read Georges Izard's *L'Homme est révolutionnaire* (Man Is Revolutionary), you'll have seen a vivid example of these difficulties.[8] Izard fails to let go of his 'common sense' [*logique*] judgement, and every step he takes together with the thinking of Marxist authors is followed — as one is followed by one's shadow — by a logical step that betrays the meaning the authors quoted had given it. The result is predictable: he understands nothing of dialectical materialism.

I don't think it needless to remind you what dialectical materialism means by 'matter'. It employs a concept of matter different to the one we are used to. In its usual conception, the quality 'matter', such as when I say, for example, that this table is matter, corresponds only to one stage in its becoming. Above all, *dialectics teaches us to conceive of everything in terms of its development*. From then on, 'spirit', 'energy', and 'matter' can no longer appear as irreducible antinomies: they are stages in the evolution of a whole, of which they are parts. For the Marxist, 'matter' is synonymous with 'objective reality' as that which exists outside our consciousness — this 'outside' being wholly relative, since consciousness itself is merely the 'reflection' of this reality.

We come now to the ideas of 'reflection' and 'consciousness', which are at the very heart of dialectical materialism's position on the problem of thought, a problem that, as you know, is central to psychiatry. We have to admit that the use of the word 'reflection' seems clumsy. We are tempted to see ideas of passivity and nothingness in it — but these senses are far removed from the thinking of Marx and of Lenin, both of whom deny consciousness *as the primary source* of the world and of itself.

---

8   Georges Izard, *L'Homme est révolutionnaire* (Paris: Grasset, 1945).

[For example,] Izard asks

> how the brain could produce sensations, ideas, reasoning, intuitions, philosophical or artistic conceptions, memory, volitions and, in general, consciousness.[9]

This is the kind of false problem that Marxists refrain from asking. Note, first, the abstract nature of the question: it does not bear on the brain of Jean, a man situated in the concrete world of his history, nor about his concrete will — for example, to go and buy the newspaper. Izard's 'will' amounts, as it were, to 'volitions' in general... I think it's worth pointing out that, although there are phrases in Marxist classics that state that thought is 'secreted' by the brain, we have no right to conceive of the old texts of Marxists as petrified objects, abstracted from their time.

By contrast, the overall meaning of dialectical materialism prevents us from taking the sentence quoted above 'at face value'. In the first place, to pose the problem in this way is to ignore the *law of reciprocal action*, according to which we must always keep in mind chains of processes, *whereby everything influences everything*; this law of development reveals to us the absolute monism that is presupposed by dialectical materialism.

Now, since the brain is an organ, it can be separated from the rest of the organism, the person, and the world for didactic purposes only. Nothing is more opposed to Marxism than the error of taking *processes in isolation*. 'Brain/thought' form a pair of phenomena that are connected through causal ties that we have no right to separate out from other determining factors. The brain is not a ready-made machine [constituted] once and for all (one

---

9   Ibid., p. 40.

of the difficulties of contemporary neurology has been to overcome the prejudice of stability concerning the brain's anatomical structures); likewise, the brain cannot act in the body as a whole *without* what we might call the 'concrete experience of the physical and social world' in which it develops.

Wallon has recently emphasized that there is a certain level of reality at which a given effect can no longer be considered the result of a single cause.[10] For some time now medicine has turned its attention to the study of *functional correlations*, and if initially it confined itself to intra-organic correlations, this was undoubtedly due to the concrete and historical approach it had adopted as regards its 'object' — the sick person affected somewhere in their organism. However, the advent of hygiene and social medicine has meant that medicine has turned its attention outwards, simultaneously introducing a new element of causal knowledge into the determinism of 'diseases': the statistical technique.

There can be no doubting the biological unity of the organism and its milieu; recently, Jemersch Roberts from the Société de Biologie recalled Howe's studies on the absence

---

10   Wallon, 'Matérialisme dialectique et psychologie', pp. 15–16: 'Matter is not made up of elements perpetually similar to themselves, whose permanent properties would immediately explain the totality of reality. [...] Change is the essential condition of being. Its becoming is a qualitative creation. These quantitative changes, when they reach a certain degree, give rise to a qualitative change. This law holds power over the evolution of being, from the atom through animal species to human societies. But it cannot be realized without an extremely diverse set of actions and reactions. Indeed, change is not due to an intimate force of transformation. It is provoked from outside, the result of an opposition that forces what exists to modify itself in order to continue to exist. The cause is external to the effect. But it is often itself the effect of what it tends to modify, for there is no existence that can develop, in isolation and for itself, without acting on the milieu and without giving rise to antagonistic forces.'

of globulins in the blood of new-born calves. The presence, specificity, and 'personal' character of blood globulins can be explained in that they are antibodies that we make throughout our lives, depending on our chance encounters and accidents, diet included. This new fact confirms the dialectical, historical, and concrete unity of our organism and its milieu, a fact that the most 'organic' medicine cannot do without. The same is true of the brain: no longer can an 'organist' have any doubts that this organ is produced throughout life's course, and that, to a certain extent, we produce it ourselves — nor can anyone ignore the significance of social and 'external' processes in general in this organ's development.

What dialectical materialism allows us to grasp is that this development takes place through 'acting' alone. Hence, anatomy need not be fully separated from physiology — today these two sciences are no longer distinct. Medicine has had to pass through this stage of knowledge and investigation bound to petrification of the object of study, and to conceive, but only *afterwards, function* as *caused* by some 'stable structure'. At this stage of medicine, on the back of the 'primitive materialisms', 'matter' was taken in the vulgar sense and seen in opposition to 'energy' and to 'action'.

Even today, a frequent oversight or misunderstanding as regards dialectical materialism arises from the 'logical' difficulties we experience when confronted with Marx's thesis that

> chief defect of all previous materialism is that the object, effectiveness, sensibility is grasped only under the form of the object or of intuition; but not as sensibly human activity, practice.[11]

---

11 Marx continues: 'This explains why the active side was always developed by idealism in opposition to materialism, but only abstractly,

Understanding this thesis requires that we have shed all anthropocentric error, have subjected such error to historical critique and have grasped, finally, in its entirety, the unity of being. The real is one, including the human being, who is therefore nature or matter: the human being's practical activity is evolved matter.[12]

The Laws of Dialectical Development are Laws of the Development of Nature

Now let's leave aside Marx's elaboration of this conception of matter, which, through the action of the 'human/nature' antithesis at the time, allowed him to glimpse a progressive, revolutionary solution. You're familiar with these develop-

---

since idealism naturally does not know effective, sensible activity as such. Feuerbach wants sensible objects — ones effectively different from objects of thought: but he does not grasp human activity itself as *objective* activity.' See *Karl Marx's Theses on Feuerbach: A New English Translation Based on the New Marx-Engels-Gesamtausgabe*, trans. by Carlos Bendaña-Pedroza, translation modified (2022) <https://www.academia.edu/42897184/Karl_Marx_s_Theses_on_Feuerbach_A_New_English_Translation_Based_on_the_New_Marx_Engels_Gesamtausgabe_By_Carlos_Bendaña_Pedroza> [accessed 8 April 2024]. For a different translation see '[Theses on Feuerbach]', trans. by the Institute of Marxism-Leninism, in *Marx & Engels Collected Works*, 50 vols (London: Lawrence and Wishart, 1975–2004), v: *Marx and Engels. 1845–1847* (1976), digital edn (2010), pp. 3–5 (p. 3): 'The chief defect of all previous materialism (that of Feuerbach included) is that the thing [*Gegenstand*], reality, sensuousness are conceived only in the form of the *object, or of contemplation*, but not as *sensuous human activity, practice*, not subjectively.' For the German text see '1) ad Feuerbach', in *Marx-Engels-Gesamtausgabe (MEGA²)* (Berlin: Akademie Verlag), IV/3: *Exzerpte und Notizen. Sommer 1844 bis Anfang 1847* (1998), pp. 19–21.

12   On the basis of this same passage from the *Theses on Feuerbach*, Wilhelm Reich laid down an open conception of dialectical materialism, one opposed to a mechanistic conception reduced to 'measurable, ponderable, and palpable matter', and favourable to the development of a materialist psychology. See his 'Dialectical Materialism and Psychoanalysis' [1934], in *Sex-Pol: Essays, 1929–1934* (London and New York: Verso, 2012), pp. 1–74.

ments, which can be found in the *Economic and Philosophic Manuscripts of 1844*.[13]

For the time being, what seems to me more 'actual' is the following point: even before we grasped human action as matter, perhaps even before we 'repressed' this conception, we were brought back to and forced to overcome many obstacles so that we could grasp the biological action of a determined organ as constitutive of the *unitary structure* of that determined organ, of its materiality. Significantly, this conviction took hold only after various techniques had enabled us to study single cell beings and microscopic anatomy. Likewise, other logical obstacles impeded the need to understand the materiality of an organ's action as *conditioned by multiple factors existing outside it*, in the organism or elsewhere.

Was this moment of scientific knowledge not indispensable in order to pass through, prior to overcoming, the

---

13   Revised note. The *Economic and Philosophic Manuscripts of 1844* were published posthumously in 1932 (as 'Ökonomisch-philosophische Manuskripte aus dem Jahre 1844 (Zur Kritik der Nationalökonomie, mit einem Schlußkapitel über die Hegelsche Philosophie)', in *Marx-Engels-Gesamtausgabe* (*MEGA¹*), 14 vols (Berlin: Marx-Engels-Verlag, 1927–40), I/3 (1932), pp. 29–172), and were partially translated into French for the first time by Jules Molitor for the edition of the *Œuvres complètes de Karl Marx* (*Œuvres philosophiques*, 57 vols (Paris: Éditions Costes, 1924–54), VI: *Économie allemande et philosophie, Idéologie allemande (1ère partie)*, trans. by Jules Molitor (1937). As the only French translation available in 1947, Tosquelles quotes from it, drawing also on his own (no doubt multilingual) 'comparative study' (see above, p. 48). For the German text see 'Ökonomisch-philosophische Manuskripte (Erste Wiedergabe)', in *Marx-Engels-Gesamtausgabe* (*MEGA²*) (Berlin: Dietz, 1975–), I/2: *Werke. Artikel. Entwürfe. März 1843 bis August 1844* (1982), pp. 187–322, and for the English translation by Martin Milligan and Dirk J. Struik, see 'Economic and Philosophic Manuscripts of 1844', in *Marx & Engels Collected Works*, 50 vols (London: Lawrence and Wishart, 1975–2004), III: *Karl Marx: March 1843–August 1844*, digital edn (2010), pp. 229–346. References to the English translation and the original German edition of the manuscripts are given using the abbreviations *MECW* and *MEGA²* respectively.

anthropocentric error as regards our personal activity in the world? I think it was. But remember this: *materialist dialectics enables us to grasp the unity of action* (physiology, if you like) *and of matter* (anatomy). The whole finalistic aspect contained in the famous phrase 'the function creates the organ' falls by the wayside. In actual fact, the function does create the organ, but the organ thus created produces actions of a different, higher order. What's more, this new organ's existence does not arise without changing the role of the anatomical-physiological structures that were at its origin. Herein lies the whole problem of integration and subordination.

Psychosomatic medicine would thus seem to find its theoretical justification. Note that for American psycho-somaticists, action, which is 'physiology/pathology', creates anatomopathological structures. Every 'action' or 'situation' bears witness to the human being's active presence in the world. 'History' is 'social physiology'. 'Action' is 'matter' (in the Marxist sense) and produces matter (in the usual sense of the word). There is no thought without a human brain, no human brain outside of the person [*hors de l'homme*], nor person outside of the world.

Thought cannot be studied in the abstract, except as part of the total nature of which it is a 'section'. The method for investigating total nature is precisely dialectical materialism. *The laws of dialectical development are the laws of the development of nature* (including the human being, the nervous system, and thought). You know them: *the interpenetration and identity of opposites*[14] *(the true driving force of development), and the dialectical reversal and transformation of quantity into quality.*

---

14   Translator's note: The French text has *contraintes* here, but it seems a mistake for *contraires*, the *identité de contraires* being the usual French expression for the dialectical operator, the identity of opposites.

In Wallon we find a differentiation — one that I think is too clear-cut — between what he calls 'individual development', which corresponds to childhood (a phenomenon linked to nervous system maturation), and the problem of adult 'knowledge' (dependent above all on historical and social conditions).[15] It's true that he is not unaware of adult society's impact [*portée*][16] on manifestations of infantile thought, thanks to which he did not succumb to over-simplistic parallelisms, such as the identifying of pre-categorical infantile thought with the magical thought of the 'primitives'. Similarly, we can assume that he doesn't reject the fact that adult knowledge is still dependent on the maturation, immaturity, or even involution of the nervous system. However, I think that this distinction (perhaps more didactic or apparent in his presentations than it is in his thinking) partly responds to the limitation of his research object, which must inevitably influence the thinking of any researcher, however 'broadly' Marxist he may be.[17]

I make this point because, opposite the 'neurological', it leads us to that other pole of factors, namely those defined as 'sociological'. The oscillation between these two poles of attraction seems to define certain psychiatric attitudes, and, just as it led Auguste Comte to deny the

---

15 See Henri Wallon, 'Science de la nature et science de l'homme: La Psychologie' [1931], *Enfance*, 12.3–4 (1959), pp. 203–19 <https://doi.org/10.3406/enfan.1959.1435>.

16 The original transcription reads: '*perte*' (loss).

17 Other obstacles are also mentioned by Wallon himself: 'Since irrefutable evidence has shown that [science] is subject, unwittingly or without wishing to admit it, to constraints or directives that are sometimes pernicious: examination or competition syllabuses, economic or military interests, ideological continuations, official tutelage, the task imposed upon us was to verify, each in their own field, the meaning and scope of the relationships that science maintains with the different orders of facts or factors of which social reality is composed.' ('Introduction', in *À la lumière du marxisme. Essais*, ed. by Henri Wallon and others (Paris: Éditions sociales internationales, 1935), pp. 9–16 (p. 10)).

possibilities of psychology,[18] it also seems to lead a certain number of psychiatrists, somewhat paradoxically, to misjudge the originality and delimitation of psychiatry's object.

First, then, we will have to define the social and the human according to dialectical materialism.

Analysis of Forms: The Social and the Human Being Through the Prism of Dialectical Materialism

Marx, in his analysis of forms (where what he calls 'alienation' is reflected in ideology and political economy), presupposes the positive abolition of private property, which gives us a clear description of the human being's social essence — 'the human being [*Mensch*] produces the human being — itself and other humans.'[19] Society is, for Marx, 'humankind's *complete* consubstantiality with nature',[20] and he urges us to take care 'to avoid postulating "society" again as an abstraction vis-à-vis the individual. The individual *is* the *social being*.'[21] 'My *own* existence is social activity': everything that I do, even if it does not reach society directly, I do as '*socially* active, because I am active as *human*'.[22]

---

18   See notably Auguste Comte, opening lesson of the *Cours de philosophie positive* [1830] (Paris: Hermann, 1998).

19   Marx consistently employs the term '*Mensch*', which in German designates a human individual without distinction of sex: 'der Mensch den Menschen producirt, sich selbst und den andern Menschen' (*MECW*, p. 297, translation modified (tm); *MEGA*^{2}, p. 264).

20   *MECW*, p. 298, tm (*MEGA*^{2}, p. 264).

21   *MECW*, p. 299 (*MEGA*^{2}, p. 267).

22   *MECW*, p. 298, tm (*MEGA*^{2}, p. 267).

> So the *social character* is the general character of
> the whole movement; *just as* society itself produces
> *humans as humans,* so is society *produced* by them.[23]

Thus, the social being is the living form of which 'my *general*
consciousness is only the *theoretical* form.'[24] Says Marx,

> much as the human person may therefore be a
> *particular* individual [...], [this person] is just
> as much the *totality* — the ideal totality — the
> subjective existence of imagined and experienced
> society for itself; just as this person exists also in
> the real world both as awareness and real enjoy-
> ment of social existence, and as a totality of human
> manifestation of life.[25]

'Thinking and being', he concludes, 'are thus certainly distinct, but at the same time they are in unity with each
other.'[26] I also find it interesting to note that a few pages
before describing the social essence of the human, Marx
sketches what we might call a dialectic from the natural
to the social that passes via psycho-sexual conduct: depending on the form that obtains in male/female relations,
he says, we see 'how far *humankind* as a *species-being,* as
humankind, has become itself and grasped itself'.[27] 'It is
possible to judge from this relationship the entire level of
development of humankind.'[28]

---

23 *MECW,* p. 298, tm (*MEGA*^{2}, p. 264).

24 Marx: 'Mein *allgemeines* Bewußtsein ist nur die *theoretische* Gestalt'
(*MECW,* p. 298; *MEGA*^{2}, p. 267).

25 Marx: 'Der Mensch — so sehr er daher ein *besondres* Individuum ist
[...] ebenso sehr ist er die *Totalität,* die ideale Totalität, das subjektive
Dasein d[er] Gedachten und empfundnen Gesellschaft für sich, wie er
auch in der Wirklichkeit, sowohl als Anschauung und wirklicher Genuß
des gesellschaftlichen Daseins, wie als eine Totalität menschlicher Le-
bensäußerung da ist' (*MECW,* p. 299, tm; *MEGA*^{2}, p. 268).

26 Marx: 'Denken und Sein sind also zwar *unterschieden,* aber zugleich in
Einheit *miteinander*' (*MECW,* p. 299; *MEGA*^{2}, p. 268).

27 *MECW,* p. 296, tm (*MEGA*^{2}, p. 262).

28 *MECW,* p. 296, tm (*MEGA*^{2}, p. 262).

The human being's alienation, which Marx assumes is due to private property and its [inter-projection],[29] fails to conceal the relationship between man and woman as 'the *most natural* relation'. So, with the 'need' for women, 'need' in general becomes 'human', and 'the other' becomes a 'need' for humans more generally.[30]

Thus, 'In their *natural* species-relationship', he says,

> the relation of humans to nature is immediately their relation to humans, just as their relation to other humans is immediately their relation to nature, their own *natural* destination.[31]

In other words, we are, it is true, nature. By positing the naturalness of humankind, we develop *relationships with form*, from which arise states of 'need' that generalize to *other humans* in general; so our natural form of living results in *society*, and society is thus [both] nature and ourselves together, that is it is *'humanized nature'*.

This development would seem to correspond perfectly with the essential findings that psychoanalysis enabled us to verify much later, it being understood that the sexual relationship that Marx envisages must be taken in the most general sense — the one he also gives it — of the 'relationship between man and woman' and, more concretely,

---

29 The original transcription indicates: 'interjection'. We could see this as a simple typo ('interjection' for 'introjection'), but here we suggest the hypothesis that Tosquelles used this term to mark the inter-human character of the process at work in the introjection of private property, which is then inscribed in the very relations as constitutive of 'the positive community', in primitive communism.

30 *MECW*, p. 296 (*MEGA*^{2}, p. 262).

31 Marx: 'In diesem *natürlichen* Gattungsverhältniß ist das Verhältniß des Menschen zur Natur unmittelbar sein Verhältniß zum Menschen wie das Verhältniß zum Menschen unmittelbar sein Verhältniß zur Natur, seine eigne *natürliche* Bestimmung ist' (*MECW*, p. 295, tm; *MEGA*^{2}, p. 262).

of the relationship, inevitably, with the mother. The same false accusation of pansexuality (part of an overly myopic interpretation) that has been levelled at Freud's writings could also be applied to this text by Marx.

In fact, he makes his thoughts clear in the sentence immediately following our last quote of his work:

> The entire movement of history is therefore the *actual* act of its generation — the birth act of its empirical existence [of the human being].[32]

Isn't the repetition of real and social existence in thought, this historical quality of the human being, the core of the conceptions that have entered the scientific investigation of 'conditional reflex learning'[33] and the 'complex'?[34]

---

32   Translator's note: The full quotes in English and German are provided below. As the reader will see, Marx speaks about the generation of communism here, whereas Tosquelles uses the dialectical structure expressed in the quote to talk about the generation of humankind. The full quote in English is: 'The entire movement of history, just as its [communism's] *actual* act of genesis — the birth act of its empirical existence — is, therefore, also for its thinking consciousness the *comprehended* and *known* process of its *becoming.*' Marx: 'Die ganze Bewegung der Geschichte ist daher, wie sein *wirklicher* Zeugungsakt — der Geburtsakt seines empirischen Daseins — so auch für sein denkendes Bewußtsein die *begriffne* und *gewußte* Bewegung seines *Werdens*' (*MECW*, p. 297; *MEGA*^{2}, p. 263).

33   Pavlov's work in the field of psychology, based especially on his knowledge of the digestive process, was promoted by the behaviourists of the time, in particular John Broadus Watson. See also below, p. 82.

34   See Jacques Lacan, *Family Complexes in the Formation of the Individual* [French original, 1938], trans. by Cormac Gallagher (London: Karnac, 2003).

PSYCHOPATHOLOGY AND PSYCHIATRY

Contradiction and Coincidence of Opposites in the Object of Psychiatry

Society, the nervous system, and the organism in general are not irreducible, isolated compartments.

If we tend to study them as separate sciences, it is because of the differentiation of the techniques we employ; so that the technique, the possibilities of human action, limit the object of each particular science, although this object itself can never be considered in abstraction from society. Marx shows us 'how the object, being the direct manifestation of the human's individuality, is simultaneously a human's own existence for the other, the existence of the other, and that existence for one'.[35]

Naturally, understanding and admitting this means that we judge based on the dialectic, that is we view causality not as a one-way movement, but instead learn to see a fact not only as the outcome of its antecedent, but also as the starting point of its cause.

An example among thousands will help you to grasp the point: the hypophysis secretes under the action of hypothalamic excitations, but hypothalamic excitations depend on pituitary secretions that, through [neurocrinia], reach the hypothalamus. Let us say in passing that this fact is not exceptional in the nervous system; indeed, Roussy

---

35   The word Marx uses is actually not *Objekt* (in French, the *objet* '*objectif*'; in English the 'objective' *object*) but *Gegenstand* — object in the sense of 'objectal', of that with which we are dealing, and which can also be of a subjective order: 'wie der Gegenstand, welcher die unmittelbare Bethätigung seiner Individualität zugleich sein eignes Dasein für den andern Menschen dessen Dasein und dessen Dasein für ihn ist' (*MECW*, p. 298, tm; *MEGA*^{2}, p. 264).

and Mosinger have successfully proven its generality.[36] Similarly, Bonnafé and Follin have reminded us at the recent Bonneval discussions that emotion can only be grasped in its dialectical structure, whereby action and re-action are intertwined to such an extent that the process of development over time can take place in both directions.[37]

However, psychiatry's object cannot be attained through abstraction: we can delimit it only through the historical succession of techniques of assistance and treatments. To some extent, paraphrasing Landsberg's existentialist definition on the topic of philosophy, we can say that psychiatry is what psychiatrists do.

So what do psychiatrists do? First of all, they are not humans standing outside the world; they are integral to their epoch and subject to its technological and social influences. There is also a history of the figure of the psychiatrist and what it does, and the point is to grasp its laws of evolution with a view to grasping the current and future state of psychiatric approaches.

The laws that govern assistance to the mentally ill, which we regard as outdated, are not entirely wrong when

---

36   See Gustave Roussy and Michel Mosinger, 'Rapports anatomiques et physiologiques de l'hypothalamus et de l'hypophyse', *Annales de médecine*, 33.3 (1933), pp. 301–24.

37   See Lucien Bonnafé and Sven Follin, 'À propos de la psychogenèse: étude critique de l'organo-dynamisme de Henri Ey: les bases d'une psychiatrie concrète, science originale de l'homme-psychopathe', in *Le Problème de la psychogenèse des névroses et des psychoses*, ed. by Henri Ey (Paris: Desclée de Brouwer, 1950; repr. Paris: Tchou, 2004), p. 142: 'Let's remember that in the facts emotion actually shows us the existence of a determinism where the cause that produces a certain effect is at the same time modified by it: the effect of some cause can also act in return on the events that first determined it. Emotive processes are characteristic of this modality of life, where the action and reaction of certain aspects on other aspects are interwoven to such an extent that the process of development over time can take place in both directions; this, we believe, is the only way to grasp the unity of the emotive structure.'

they define — as public opinion continues to — madness in terms of internment.[38] And in the struggle between the position defended by Heuyer and his pupils and that argued for by Daumézon, Bonnafé, and all the doctors of non-conformist asylums,[39] we should see *the contradiction and coincidence of opposites* in the process of developing the therapeutic and techniques of assistance that psychiatry uses.

Naturally, the phenomenon of *object evolution* is not specific to psychiatry — although, in this sector of human action, it does take on particular characteristics. The object of chemistry, for example, has not been defined in isolation from its evolution. It emerged from alchemy and its

---

38 These assistance laws, still in force in 1947, date from 1848. The first volume of Documents de *L'Information psychiatrique* (Paris: Desclée de Brouwer, 1946) was devoted to giving an overview of the subject, together with a report by Daumézon ('La Protection de la santé mentale en France. État actuel et projets de rénovation', pp. 9–77) and an article by Bonnafé and Daumézon ('L'Internement, conduite primitive de la société devant la maladie mentale: recherche d'une attitude plus évoluée', pp. 79–107). Daumézon also offers a glimpse into the climate of crisis in 'Crise de recrutement... Crise de la psychiatrie', *L'Information psychiatrique*, 7 (1947). In the journal's same issue, Henri Ey had published 'Un projet de réglementation de l'exercice de la psychiatrie'.

39 Revised note. Jean-Christophe Coffin sheds light on this opposition in his article 'Un syndicat en psychiatrie: une association d'intérêt?', in *Syndicats et associations: concurrence ou complémentarité?*, ed. by Danielle Tartakowsky and Françoise Tétard (Rennes: Presses universitaires de Rennes, 2015), pp. 139–47. Georges Daumézon headed an alliance of psychiatrists around the journal *L'Évolution psychiatrique,* close to the Syndicat des médecins des hôpitaux psychiatriques (which would thereafter become affiliated with the CGT [General Confederation of Labour, which was the biggest national trade union confederation in France at the time and had close ties to the French Communist Party]) in favour of a so-called social psychiatry. But in 1947, a lively debate took place within the union 'on the pertinence of classifying certain patients as chronic, with the risk that these patients are turned into social rejects'. Once again, the discussion revolved around the very object of psychiatry itself. In 1951, Georges Heuyer founded the Syndicat des médecins français du système nerveux.

relationship with the techniques employed as part of the pursuit of the fantasy of the philosopher's stone. Of course, the fantasy object of alchemy does not define the object of chemistry, but the latter was in fact delimited within a sector of the real through the evolution of techniques of alchemical origin.

Even classical medicine is no exception to this general evolutionary law, and here, as in chemistry, we find a return to primitive positions, but, on another level, this time stripped of mythology (the spiralling evolution of dialectical materialism):

Primitive physicians — if we can refer to the sorcerer in this way — called on all the world's 'magical or divine forces' to heal the sick; they practised incantations, collective rites, and so on.

Today's physicians call on the state — for example, they call for scientific urban planning to cure and prevent tuberculosis; they rally around the Comité national des médecins français to perform social rites aimed at equipping the country with sanitary facilities, without which there can be no scientific medicine... But please do note: this time the approach is not part of a mystification.

The Object of Psychiatry: Affirmation or Negation

The integration of so-called organic diseases into society is the consequence of the most careful scientific research and experimentation — a development of the position taken and defined by Claude Bernard, and, if you will, its antithesis.

To see the evolution of psychiatry's object, we need only look back at its history. In fact, the problem of the extension and delimitation of psychiatry's object has been clearly brought to the attention of most of us during our current *Journées psychiatriques nationales*:[40] 'With what are we going to be occupied?' my colleagues have asked themselves. 'Mad people? Neurotics? Career guidance? Conflicts of character that erupt within households? Criminals?' Have we not even foreseen the possibility that we will necessarily find ourselves becoming 'technical advisors' to the public authorities on a host of problems of propaganda and political opportunism — such as finding out the opinion of the masses, and so on?[41] The fact of madness seems to be defined by a 'disturbance of thought' and of 'belief'. But let's not be too hasty in seeing this fact in isolation from the overall factors that condition it: the aim of medicine is precisely to act with efficacy against the factors that condition the concrete morbid event.

Psychiatrists had it put to them to *change the conducts and beliefs* of certain persons that society had conceived as 'the sick' — first we were told that these people were sick in the brain. Psychiatrists thus studied the brain. In keeping with this thesis, psychiatrists developed the reputed mythology of brain localizations, a mythology that — let us note — opens the way to its antithesis: the mythology

---

40   The proceedings of the 1947 *Journées psychiatriques nationales* are published in *L'Information psychiatrique* nos. 6 (March 1947) and 7 (May 1947). These questions would arise again at the 1947 London Congress, and shaped the policy of the recently established World Health Organization (WHO), with the notable creation of the World Federation for Mental Health.

41   Tosquelles points to a possible excess of psychiatry with the development on demand of psychometric tests — sometimes motivated, on the pretext of vocational guidance, by the need to improve selection to increase worker productivity. His criticism of a possible excess is underpinned by his own training in the use of psychometric tests with Emilio Mira [y López], at Barcelona's Institutio de Orientación Professional (Institute of Vocational Guidance), now the Institute de Psicotécnica (Psychotechnical Institute). But the comments transcribed in the following paragraphs undoubtedly earned him the opposition of some audience members.

of speculations about the soul or its guises.[42] At issue here is thus a real return to the medieval conception and the mythology of possessions; a mythology that the notion of the 'mad-patient' [*fou-malade*] contested through its act of seeking to establish itself.

As a science of observation rather than experimentation (a path Claude Bernard had already concluded was the 'constancy of the development of any science'), French psychiatry, which was the most scientific psychiatry of the time, classified the various types of madness, drew up catalogues, specified the facts observed, and created a seemingly concrete nosology.[43] To the credit of French psychiatry, it refused to follow the antithetical movement that, for reasons that would take too long to explain, was developing in Germany, where psychiatrists were engaging in a non-dialectical evolutionism and making sweeping nosological syntheses. Classical German conceptions were turned into psychopathological syntheses based on the abstraction of a 'primary' and 'isolated psychis'.[44] As history has confirmed, this movement, which passes through the vicissitudes of schizophrenia and manic-depressive psychosis, leads to the comical discovery that madness is one, and is called madness.

---

42   Phrenology was promoted in particular by Auguste Comte, in conjunction with the work of anatomists such as Xavier Bichat, Henri Marie Ducrotay de Blainville, Georges Cuvier, and Franz Joseph Gall.

43   Henri Ey's organo-dynamism thesis (which has its origins partly in his 1926 translation of Eugen Bleuler's work on the psychopathology of schizophrenia) is an alternative to the 'positivist' positions described above.

44   Karl Jaspers was reputedly hostile to evolutionary theories, and claimed the need to make room for 'understanding' alongside naturalistic 'explanation'. See *General Psychopathology* [German original, 1913], trans. by J. Hoenig and Marian W. Hamilton (Baltimore, MD: John Hopkins University Press, 1997).

On the one hand, French psychiatry is to be credited, but on the other, there is a marking of time… In science, unlike philosophy, you must know how to wait!

What doesn't wait, however, are patients and the pressing need for medical action: through trial and error, through the purest empiricism, techniques and therapeutics follow one another and, along the way, present us with new problems. It's in trying to solve these problems that new techniques are discovered. In this way, a dialectic of thought, experience, techniques, and object is established, in which each part conditions the whole, and the whole conditions each part.

The Dialectic in Psychiatry, or Searching for Possibilities of Action

The dialectical method, however, needs to pose its problems in a concrete way, and medicine is an art that always brings us back to the real, even when physicians or patients may slip into a more or less traditional mythology.

The problems of madness, as we experience them in the clinic, are never posed in the abstract: hallucinations, thoughts, feelings, emotions, delirium… What we find, 'our object', is a sick person with such and such a history (pathological or not), in such and such a situation, who talks and behaves in such and such a way: the practice of medicine is one of concrete people, and not a nosological pursuit of abstractions. Analysis and medical synthesis must be undertaken anew with each new case. At issue is to search for deterministic reference points (!), for possibilities of action, and not to label patients. If psychiatrists continue to mark time through this absurd nosographic search, we ought to see it as part of the conditioning undergone in the very fact of internment: no one, or practically no one, asks them to cure; they are asked to put a label on, to sanction, above all, a social measure.

Bonnafé recently coined a felicitous phrase in which he describes the medical work that needs doing as a 'dis-alienation of the total fact of madness': the sick person, the asylum, *and* the psychiatrist at once.[45] Without wanting to state that psychiatrists are mad, it is true that the conditions under which they practise their profession (shut away with their patients in the asylum) have alienated them from society as a whole, and divorced them even from medicine.

If one of the patient's primary manifestations indeed consists in some anomaly of thought, belief, and action, dialectical materialism forbids examining only the processual chain that seems to be directly linked to these disorders. We must consider all the processes (the greatest number in any case) that are open to observation, and first and foremost the patient's particular history and development, their concrete situation in the world, and the 'ergo-neurological' dissolutions the patient presents. But the psychiatrist's synthesis will not be constructed entirely out of their own thinking. It can only be a reproduction, a

---

45   Bonnafé's oral report to the *Journées psychiatriques nationales* on 27 and 28 January 1947, on the 'Conception moderne d'un établissement de cure et de réadaptation' ('Modern Conception of a Treatment and Rehabilitation Establishment'), which he would later evoke in 'Le Personnage du psychiatre' ('The Figure of the Psychiatrist'): 'Strictly considering the aim pursued, namely the effectiveness of our action in disalienating the psychiatric fact, patient, care organization, doctor, we are allowed to work out well-considered conducts. As prudent strategists, on the basis of a thorough study of the conditions of the problem, i.e., above all the situation of the psychiatric fact in society, we have to define our character, adapt it to our ends, conceive with this in mind propaganda plans, even battle plans, in which for example the rational use of our resentment against a hostile world can be skilfully exploited, releasing under strict control a part of our reactive aggression. But for this, our own analysis is a prerequisite. The usual lack of serenity in our reactions can only be corrected on this condition' (*L'Évolution psychiatrique*, 13.3 (1948), pp. 23–56).

reflection of the real. We mustn't forget that this object is already synthetic, homogeneous, or global at the level of the real, in the form of pathological behaviour; the particular behaviour of a person in a concrete social situation, a situation that has a meaning for them.

When Marxist psychiatrists like Bonnafé and Follin ask what dissolution of function is involved in the alienated human, they respond by saying that this dissolution merely reflects a transformation of social life, proposed to a particular individual in a given milieu and at a given historical moment. The 'psychopath' is thus an isolated individual, and they envisage this individual, following Georges Politzer, as a social phenomenon made up of concatenations and linkages of sectors that comprise the 'concrete drama' thus lived.[46]

We've already seen how, for the Marxist, the social phenomenon is consubstantial with the human being, and is just as natural as madness or this table. It therefore seems legitimate, according to dialectical materialism, to contemplate the social phenomenon that the psychopathic human being is. Moreover, this way of conceiving things can be expected to produce a salutary break with the isolation we 'unravelled' above among psychiatrists themselves.

Since theory is only as good as the action it enables, Marxist psychiatrists maintain a clear, definite, and coherent position on this subject:

• Their aim is therapeutic action with an awareness of its social structure and scope, social therapy, and the conversion

---

46   'The psychopathic individual is a fact both global and original. All modern psychiatric research is the search for a method that takes into account both this originality and this totality, which until now has been prevented from being grasped only by the persistence of metaphysical thinking.' (Sven Follin, 'Rationalisme moderne et psychiatrie', *L'Évolution psychiatrique*, [13].4 (1948), p. 126).

of the asylum into a social milieu of different levels, foregrounded by therapy through work — both social therapy and simple classical psychotherapy, which is one of the effective forms of the doctor/patient social relationship.

• In another aspect, the social therapy they undertake grasps each concrete case, works close to the patient's family and the milieu they will be returned to, and perhaps also, on a general level, this social therapy aims, in line with the political aims of Marxism, at the human being's disalienation.

This position is an extraordinarily coherent one, and among most non-Marxist practitioners is rarely found.

Concrete Psychiatry: Unity of Conceptions and of Practices

I don't have time to go into each and every psychiatric work that displays the banner of dialectical materialism. In fact, it has to be said that there is no point in examining them, since dialectical materialism will 'absorb' any scientifically founded work *a posteriori*. Nevertheless:

• There are authors who put forward Marxist conceptions in their scientific work. Let's recall Wilhelm Reich, who undertook a critique of the Freudian death drive based on psychoanalytic practice,[47] and Georges Politzer who engaged in a wide-ranging theoretical critique of psychoanalysis in general.[48]

47　See Wilhelm Reich, 'The Masochistic Character' [German original, 1932], in *Character Analysis* [German original, 1933], trans. by Vincent R. Carfagno and ed. by Mary Higgins and Chester M. Raphael (New York: Farrar, Straus and Giroux, 1980), pp. 225–69.

48　Tosquelles's library included the first (and only) two issues of the *Revue de psychologie concrète*, dated 1928 and 1929 respectively. Georges Politzer writes, in the Editorial of no. 1, 'Les Fondements de la psychologie' (pp. 1–8): 'In particular, it will be a question of examining

• Russian authors, presumably Marxist, have produced works of unequal importance. We can cite, for example, studies on the experimental 'cyclothymization'[49] of schizoids given work as sellers. With the application of statistical methods to the research of occupational diseases, they have described a certain correlation, which can only be causal, between auditory hallucinations and work in textile factories. But they made their mark above all in the experimental development of conditional reflexes… You'll forgive me for not going into the conceptions of Pavlov and his pupils here.

Their theoretical expressions are not devoid, it should be noted, of a mechanistic and non-dialectical materialism. The result is unsurprisingly that, as we saw with Lentz's experiments, the theory of conditional reflexes in humans — taken in isolation from the dialectical whole of the historical human being in the world — led, after passing through the mythological stage of combining super-reflexes, to an undisguised return to an antinomic, dualistic opposition between the psyche-social milieu (dynamic and creative) and the stereotypical tropisms of instincts and conditional reflexes (inert and 'organic'). The Marxist deficit of this

---

the current theoretical structure of psychoanalysis, which, after a great boom, has now reached a period of stagnation. This is perhaps due to the fact that psychoanalytic research is trapped in inadequate theoretical constructs. With this in mind, we are opening a permanent chapter devoted to the crisis of psychoanalysis' (p. 5). See also his *Critique of the Foundations of Psychology: The Psychology of Psychoanalysis* [French original, 1928], trans. by Maurice Apprey (Pittsburgh, PA: Duquesne University Press, 1994). Influenced by the Communist Party's line on psychoanalysis, Politzer abandoned this work ('La Fin de la psychanalyse' [1939], in *Écrits 2. Les Fondements de la psychologie* (Paris: Éditions sociales, 1973)). Politzer was shot by the Nazis in 1942.

49   Translator's note: Tosquelles here seems to be referring to an experiment that sought to induce a sort of 'circular insanity' or 'cyclothymization' in schizoids by giving them jobs as sellers, perhaps with the therapeutic intention of making them more socially receptive.

Soviet author already appeared evident from his article published in *L'Encéphale* in 1935[50] — which, incidentally, does not detract from the scientific value of his experiments.

• Paradoxically, it was Follin in France that, on the strength of 'the consubstantiality of the human and society', went in search of the concrete social dramas that psychopaths *are*. Note that I say 'that psychopaths themselves *are*', and not [the dramas] they experience, or into which they sink: that would be to oppose the human and society, a non-Marxist position.

At this place a few days ago, you heard Follin describing the drama of the 'domestic torturers' (whom he defined, together with Dublineau, in a gestaltist and Marxist way), and the drama of the 'old maid' who lived in a closed milieu with her mother, as he expounded at length in *L'Évolution psychiatrique*.[51] I won't come back to this. It would be wrong to see Follin's studies as merely rehashing problems already much studied by German psychiatry: namely, Kraepelin's 'situational psychoses' and 'relational psychoses' (psychoses of widowed mothers-in-law), 'Kretschmer's sensory delusions' (of old maids), the paranoid reactions of the deaf, blind, etc., Ferdière's prison psychoses or 'responsibility psychoses'... It is the coherent the-

---

50 See Alexander K. Lentz, 'Les Réflexes conditionnels salivaires chez l'homme sain et aliéné et leur rapprochement avec les données de la conscience' [Salivary Conditional Reflexes in Man, Sane and Insane, and their Association with Consciousness] and Ivan Pavlov, 'Essai d'une interprétation physiologique de la paranoïa et de la névrose obsessionnelle', *L'Encéphale*, 30.2 (1935), pp. 394–440 and pp. 381–93. The English translation of Pavlov's essay is published as 'An Attempt at a Physiological Interpretation of Obsessional Neurosis and Paranoia', *Journal of Mental Science*, 80.329 (1934), pp. 187–97 <https://doi.org/10.1192/bjp.80.329.187-a>.

51 See Sophie Lesage, 'Note to the Reader on "Psychopathology and Dialectical Materialism"', in this volume, note 10, p. 43.

oretical position that enables Follin to develop another perspective for these — otherwise well-known — facts, and that makes it possible to envisage a similarly coherent therapeutics, or even the first steps of a mental hygiene approach.

If we stick to the letter of his reports, and if we wish to see his research as exhausting the problematic of his patients, Follin's position may seem inadequate. In his studies of exogenous reaction psychoses, Bonhoeffer had insisted on the intermediate toxic level between the situation and the psychic reaction — a toxic level that would determine, for example, the oneirism of Follin's patient.[52] Follin deliberately left aside all the chains of biological or even psychological (in the psychoanalytical sense) processes, limiting himself to a description of the psychiatric fact in its originality.

The merit of Follin's position lies in his delineation of the morbid event and his definition of the psychopath as 'cut off' [*isolé*], while describing a 'quality' peculiar to alienation, always remains in the concrete. We are not 'cut off' in general, but the family and the psychopath can find themselves in isolation, the psychopath faces a situation of isolation from the surrounding social milieu.

Now, there's a big difference between this position and Kronfeld's. For example, Kronfeld 'theoretically' 'understands' the neuropath's regression from 'the person' (social) to 'the individual' (the individual being something original, more 'oneself'). Here, 'individual' and 'person' are two words, two 'ideas', two 'essences'. The regression does not occur at the concrete level of the patient's life, but at

---

52 See Karl Bonhoeffer, 'Die exogenen Reaktionstypen', *Archiv für Psychiatrie und Nervenkrankheiten*, 58 (1917), pp. 58–70 <https://doi.org/10.1007/BF02036408>.

the level of the doctor's 'ideas', in their abstractions. This is why Kronfeld accepts that the psychiatrist's activity has to be split between two radically opposed attitudes: that of the practitioner, who will use the concrete techniques of psychopathology, and that of the scientist who, needing conceptions, will call upon the totality of the patient's personal 'structures'.[53] His concept of regression at the individual structural level — similar to Blondel's 'pure lived experience'[54] — is a conceptual regression, unable to be seized upon by psychiatric *praxis*.

Follin's regression presupposes the possibility of therapeutic action: there is then a *unity of conception and practice* that leads to *effectivity* (Marx says somewhere that what acts is true).[55]

• In many authors we find a social conception of personality. But more often than not, society is set *before* the individual in an abstract, non-dialectical fashion. In Janet, the social and the evolutionary are the two main ideas of its remarkable analyses; but a close methodological critique

---

53   See Arthur Kronfeld, *Das Wesen der psychiatrischen Erkenntnis* (Berlin: Julius Springer, 1920).

54   See Charles Blondel, 'Quelques réflexions sur la schizophrénie', *Travaux de la clinique psychiatrique de la faculté de Médecine de Strasbourg*, 9 (1931), pp. 7–42.

55   'Marx believed that there is a sure way of recognizing the true from the false, and that is through action. There is proof that the antinomies of reason do indeed correspond to the antinomies of reality, and that is that reason, translated into action, achieves its ends, succeeds in transforming reality [...] Theory and practice merge: only that which succeeds is true, only that which is true succeeds.' (René Maublanc, 'Hegel et Marx', in *À la lumière du marxisme. Essais*, ed. by Henri Wallon and others (Paris: Éditions sociales internationales, 1935) pp. 189–232 (pp. 224–25)). See the *Theses on Feuerbach*, where Marx writes in particular: 'The question whether objective truth can be attributed to human thinking is not a question of theory but is a *practical* question. Man must prove the truth — i.e. the effectiveness and power, the this-sidedness of his thinking in practice.' tm.

of his work would easily bring out the abstract, finalist, and dualistic aspect that will undoubtedly prevent it from being taken in 'en bloc' by dialectical materialism. The therapeutic action that can be based on Janet's work is (probably due to its abstract nature) very limited.

It seems useful here to contrast this great psychologist with someone whose analyses and conceptions seem to carry much less weight, are less subtle, and less penetrating: I have in mind Adolph Meyer's work, which, in a practical, less cultural, less theoretical, more American way, focusses on the concrete cases of these 'psychopaths' as social phenomena. The outcome of his work was a *remarkable* initiative, not only in terms of the doctor/patient relationship, but also of the social struggle represented by the work of mental hygiene.

• Finally, it would be wrong not to mention Lacan, whose doctoral thesis sets out a concrete, social-historical conception of personality that seems to reflect the essential ideas of dialectical materialism. We have recently taken up his concept of the 'complex' and his phenomenology of the doctor/patient relationship in the course of psychoanalysis, which responds to the same development of ideas.[56]

---

56   See the synthesis of works of the Société du Gévaudan signed Lucien Bonnafé, André Chaurand, François Tosquelles, and André Clément (of Saint-Alban): 'Note sur l'originalité du pathologique d'après la psychanalyse et sur la valeur du complexe comme perspective structurale dans l'existence pathologique', *Annales médico-psychologiques*, 104.2 (1946), pp. 58–63 (p. 61): 'Lacan employs a conception of the complex that is both broad and concrete. In a horizontal cross-section, the complex is a synthetic vision of a set of reactions of various kinds to a determinate, personal situation, a real 'slice of life' of the kind Politzer calls for in concrete psychology. [...] In vertical sections, centred on humankind's becoming, the complex is objectified and embodied in new situations. It expresses and realizes itself according to the possibilities of the development achieved and the social milieu in which the subject is successively placed.'

CONCLUSIONS

Materialist Monism

Let's now try to condense and summarize how and why dialectical materialism is applicable to psychopathology.

First, there is a question of principle. Similar to the medical crisis of Claude Bernard's time, the psychiatric crisis has made psychiatrists see that their scientific approaches rest on preconceptions of a philosophical nature, and some authors have not hesitated, undaunted by possible accusations of philosophical verbalism, to apprehend the philosophy that their approaches subscribe to — it has rightly been maintained that knowing 'one's' philosophy is better than to go on not knowing it. Monakow, Mourgue, Minkowski, and this series of lectures all stand in attestation to this.

But here you have to choose: are you a dualist or a monist? If you're a monist, you're either an idealist or a materialist. Dialectical materialism naturally presupposes the choice of a materialist monism: this is the path of science.

Methodology

Let us now sum up the essential features of this methodology:

• *First, the concrete object of psychiatry is not to be lost sight of: the doctor-patient interrelationship within a (no less concrete) structure of society, at a given level of its evolution.* Hence, on the one hand, the historical analysis of the 'doctor-patient' couple, and, on the other, the constant awareness, during the course of medical intervention, of the following fact: at any given moment, the 'hanging' (the *accrochage* referred to by Lagache) and the set of doctor-patient social relations are inevitably, not a situation 'external' to the sick person (beyond our practical and scientific interest), but their *situation*, that is *the person themself*, the being who needs to be cured.

Balvet, who remains uninfluenced by Marxist thought, has interestingly just published an essay in *Documents* on what might be called the 'phenomenology of the alienist', which looks at the same facts in a different language.[57] We wonder, if it weren't so, how the very possibility of psychotherapy could be grasped: it would be a 'magical' fact produced by a 'sorcerer'. But this is not the case. On this subject, Lacan has given the most complete description and analysis of the phenomena of transference and the successive identifications of which the doctor is the 'provocative-support' during the process of a psychoanalysis.

• *Second, do not isolate the processes* that the various techniques detect in the sick person, and *consider all possible intercorrelations* without limiting yourself to the fact that the processes examined are of a heterogeneous order. On the contrary, *look for fertile moments in this heterogeneity where transformations from quantity to quality take place;* look for other means of exploration among the field of techniques that allow us to examine the patient without dissolving them into functions, *techniques that are themselves polyvalent.* I have in mind the Rorschach test,[58] for example, which to a certain extent enables us to orient ourselves at once around how to establish social relationships, around the functional state of the 'ergo-nerve machine', around affective and intellectual adaptation capacities, and around the unveiling of typical complexual situations.

---

57   See Paul Balvet, 'De l'autonomie de la profession psychiatrique', in *Au-delà de l'asile d'aliénés et de l'hôpital psychiatrique*, Documents de *L'Information psychiatrique* (Paris: Desclée de Brouwer, 1946).

58   See Hermann Rorschach, *Psychodiagnostics: A Diagnostic Test Based on Perception* [German original, 1921] (Bern: Hans Huber, 1942).

• On the other hand, we need to be attentive, and *to know how to look for the antithetical elements in presence in each process*. I don't have time for a general review of these antithetical pairs; they can be found at every level of our investigation. Every practitioner is familiar with them: the coexistence or return of the repressed in the symptom, 'irritability/paralysis', 'inhibition/excitation', 'love/hate', 'sadism/masochism', amphotony of the vegetative nervous system, and so on. Let us not forget the following:

- that the concrete object we grasp and must try to transform is the *result of the convergence of multiple processes* that can overdetermine it causally or *render it indeterminate by converting causality into probability.*

- that the set of these processes finds its unity in the patient's social action, and that the patient's concrete society is itself the sick individual.

- the dialectical nature of the evolution of any process, so that the 'effect' can act on the 'cause' at the same time as the 'cause' acts on the 'effect'. At each point, we need to study not only the evolution of the fact, but also the evolution of our knowledge about the fact in question. Among the reciprocal influences at play in the evolution of a process, we must consider *the fact which we are studying and how we are studying it.* This is done not to posit a sterilizing subjectivism (reminiscent of the primacy of consciousness), but because matter consists in *praxis* (which brings us to the operationalism of the behaviourists).[59] *This*

---

59   Pierre Naville devoted an essay to this topic in 1942. See Pierre Naville, *La Psychologie, science du comportement: Le Béhaviorisme de Watson*, rev. edn (Paris: Gallimard, 1963).

> *'subjective'* [element] *is no longer ungraspable, but a concrete process.*

- the material character of the sick person's conduct, which is *conducted in the world.* There is no such thing as an antinomy between exterior and interior. So, let's not invent from scratch a second, higher ideal being, *different from what they are through their acting in the world.*

• Finally, it goes without saying that *every process must be considered in its evolution.* Dialectical materialism does not suppose originality. It even presents itself as the possible development of science in its development. Here, if you were looking to it for a metaphysics, you'd say: it has a good game, it has a captative attitude, it picks up on the work of others and can thus appear at once as gestaltist and genetic, as behaviourist and psychoanalytic, or as neurologist, all while taking account of objective lived experience!

Science is prohibited from disregarding any solidly established fact of experience; hence the highly developed critical attitude and even, in Bonnafé's apt phrase, real 'intellectual terrorism'[60] that exists in the Marxist psychiatrist — an attitude that, however, can only be fruitful alongside effective work as part of concrete medical undertakings: clinical and laboratory investigation. Here we come to an idea that Claude Bernard has expressed very clearly:

> While I accept *specialization* for what is practical
> in science, I absolutely reject it for everything that

---

60 Revised note. The phrase that Tosquelles here attributes to Bonnafé could not be located. However, the editor of the French publication places this expression in the context of Bonnafé's 'Le Personnage du psychiatre' and his oral report at the *Journées psychiatrique nationales* in 1947, referring specifically to note 45 on p. 72.

> is theoretical. Indeed, I consider that making generalities one's specialty is an anti-philosophical and anti-scientific principle.[61]

Or again:

> We'll never be able to make truly fruitful and enlightening generalizations about vital phenomena until we've experienced for ourselves, whether in the hospital, amphitheatre, or laboratory, the fetid or quivering terrain of life.[62]

Scientific Progress

The risk of Marxism — and I don't mean that all Marxists succumb to it — is precisely that this critical attitude is allowed to develop excessively, to the detriment of action or experimentation.

Medical progress, and scientific progress in general (the Marxist will agree, and, once again, Claude Bernard has said so) is measured by the perfection of their means of investigation. *In this respect, dialectical materialism, as a general conception of the world, can directly contribute little:* the transformation of means of assistance, in-depth investigation. The work of the future, like that of the past, lies above all in the patient hands of scientists who do not claim any coherent conception of the world, or who display conceptions opposed to dialectical materialism.

However, the conquests they make will be assimilated by dialectical materialism, since dialectical materialism, by definition, can have no limits on this side. I repeat that *there can be no application of Marxist philosophical principles to*

---

61   Bernard, *Introduction à l'étude de la médecine expérimentale*, p. 69.
62   Ibid., p. 54.

science as it is usually understood — in the way, for example, that scholasticism might apply to it.

Izard is right (but this does not represent a condemnation of Marxism), when he says that 'Materialism accepts being founded on holes, under the pretext that these holes correspond to the present inadequacies of scientific explanation.'[63] Or rather, he's not quite right, because it's not on holes that materialism is founded, but on science itself: it fills the holes like a bridge. Only when seen from above may the bridge appear to be based on holes — that was the opinion of a child who once remarked it to me while looking at the Garabit viaduct.

We see another pitfall that, in practice, many so-called Marxists seem to come up against: our habit of isolating social processes from the individual's set of biophysical behaviours.

As we have seen, our field seems definable at the level of the dialectic of biophysical and social behaviours. But the militant Marxist (who, let's not forget, aims at the total disalienation of the human being through the abolition of private property) finds themself the pioneer of the scientific categorization of society and may thereby suffer a kind of *déformation professionelle*.

Let's not forget that the humanization of nature and the consubstantiality of society and the human *is not an entirely current fact*. It is, according to Marx, *a state to be conquered*. And while we doctors are not forbidden to look, aspire, and fight for the future, we must live in the concrete, real present given by our patients. Carried along by an impetus that is, moreover, highly laudable, we may sometimes reach the point of mechanically applying some (or all) of the 'principles' we have described to 'present' reality — by

---

63   Izard, *L'Homme est révolutionnaire*, p. 45.

which I mean to any sick person and any situation. This is important with regard to truths detectable in social structures, as they *are* certain psychopathic events, and above all with regard to the therapeutics this discovery seemingly justifies.

In the meantime (especially when we are fighting to achieve the human being's disalienation as envisaged by Marx), we must not blindly apply measures, or even certain *psycho-social therapies*, [likely to] produce lamentable effects *at the present time* — like the doctor who refrains from operating in certain cases; we must also refrain from intervening in the course of certain psychotherapies. The rule of our art must always be *primum non nocere* (first, do no harm). There are many scientific truths that are harmful to the individual... Therapeutics is opportunism.

Naville recently made an observation that may be excessive in certain specific cases, but that at least reveals one of the risks we feel we must flag. He invited Marxist authors 'to concern themselves less with the history of philosophy, less with definitions of dialectical materialism, and a little more with particular sciences'.[64] He sees it as paradoxical (wrongly, in my opinion) that real scientific progress, that is the discovery of new dialectical processes, is rather the work of non-Marxist scholars, 'while Marxist authors content themselves with philosophical generalities, become curators of formulas and not inventors of living forms'.[65] It can't be otherwise, given society's current level of development. It is, if you like, a paradox that can be explained by dialectical materialism.

It's true, however, that the issue is to 'supersede' the contradiction rather than to explain it.

---

64   Naville, *Psychologie, marxisme, matérialisme*, p. 221
65   Ibid.

Social Being Is the Becoming of the Human, Which Is Itself

Finally, I'd like to clarify what seems to me the main idea behind the Marxian conception of the human. As we have seen, no justification can be given for opposing anatomy and physiology at the level of organs. Rather, physiology ought to be conceived as the becoming of the organ's very being. We need to conceive of the dialectical transformations of anatomical structures and functions. Similarly, at the level of the human's total structure, its physiology is action, the social situation, the social being.

Social being is the human's becoming; it is the human 'itself'. The human being and society cannot be opposed: [their] relations are dialectical. Society makes the human being, and the human being makes society. The global, non-mystified being is the human's concrete being. The psychopath is the psychopathic social being.

The originality of madness can only be defined at the level where it is, where it shows itself, in society. The determinism of madness is something else: it presupposes a chain of diverse processes, of different orders. But, I repeat, madness cannot lie otherwise than where it lies — in the behaviour of the total human being, of the social individual.

It remains to be seen whether this dialectic of society and the human being, this consubstantiality, holds today. I think Marx considers it to be 'alienated'. For him, this con-substantiality is rather a state to be conquered — which obviously limits the scope and possibilities of his conception. The fact remains, however, that insofar as the human being becomes aware of their social becoming, medicine as a whole undergoes a revolution comparable to Harvey's discovery of animal anatomy, and madness and disorders of social behaviour pass from the realm of mystery to that of science. At the same time, psychiatrists, as alienated beings in today's medicine, find their place in medicine itself: in the art of healing.

TRANSLATED BY STEVEN CORCORAN

Institutional Psychotherapy
From Saint-Alban to La Borde
JEAN OURY

INSTITUTIONAL PSYCHOTHERAPY

I am quite self-conscious about presenting 'institutional psychotherapy'; since its birth in France, it has undergone many variations — so many that its understanding is now, according to the region, according to the establishment, one of heterogeneity and full of contradictions. I will give a brief, wholly incomplete history based on my personal experience: according to the practice in which they are involved, everyone develops conceptions in their own way that become more or less theoretical after a certain number of years.

I came to the field of psychiatry in 1947 (because it is essentially a question of psychiatry when we speak of institutional psychotherapy, although its scope has been extended to other disciplines such as pedagogy or education). 1947 was still the post-war period — it is very important to underline this: institutional psychotherapy in fact has deep roots in everything that happened during the occupation. I was in the psychiatric hospital of Saint-Alban: a hospital in Lozère, lost, isolated. Perhaps owing to this isolation, an experiment had been going on for several years: the structure of this hospital had changed in a way that was quite extraordinary for the time.

How to define, even provisionally, institutional psychotherapy? The term 'institutional therapy' was often used. It meant making the most of the existing structures in order to try to take advantage of everything that could be used to care for [*soigner*] the patients [*malades*] who lived there. 'Care'?[1] The very concept of psychiatric care [*soin*] will be challenged in the development of institutional psychiatry. This movement has developed around doctors and nurses. Hospitals generally maintained a car-

---

1   Translators' note: Oury uses the French verb *soigner*, which is slightly different from the English 'care' and derives from another tradition. The verb has different meanings including 'taking care', 'treating', and 'healing', but also connotes a strong attention towards something or someone. Furthermore, he and Tosquelles use the term 'sick' or 'ill people' (*les malades*), which we mostly chose to translate as 'patients'. Historically, in the French context, the two words are not interchangeable. *Patient*, sticking with its Latin origin, refers to the one who suffers and has a connotation of passivity. Also, the word implies a position in regards to the health system and professionals: a person taken in charge by the health apparatus. In contrast, *malade* refers rather to the subjective experience (and worldview implied by this state) of the suffering individual and is also someone who can have an active role in taking care of others. As Tosquelles emphasizes: 'Psychotic and neurotic ill persons [*les malades psychotiques et les névrosés*] cannot be reduced "by their illness" to human passivity, a passivity that is, moreover, quite relative, this bracketing or resting of activity and initiative that makes ill persons [*les malades*] in internal medicine and surgery be called "patients" [*patients*]' (François Tosquelles, *Le Travail thérapeutique à l'hôpital psychiatrique* (Paris: Éditions du Scarabée, 1967), p. 13; republished as *Le Travail thérapeutique en psychiatrie* (Toulouse: Érès, 2015)). Today, there is a transnational patients' rights movement that is ascribing more agency to our understanding of who a patient is.

ceral, concentrationary structure. Now, nurses had been prisoners during the war; some had been in concentration camps... When they returned, they had a different world view: their work milieu, the same as before the war, reminded them of the experience they had just gone through.

It is an event, in a person's life, to return to their prewar profession and find themselves in a similar atmosphere to that of the concentration camps! You also know that during the occupation, there was such misery in psychiatric hospitals in France that 40 percent of the patients died of starvation. All this created a fairly favourable ground for a raising of awareness not only individually, but collectively, implying the need to change something. I like to recall this origin of institutional psychotherapy: there is often too much of a tendency to dilute everything in rather abstract, supposedly theoretical things, and ultimately lose the essence of the issue. We could therefore define institutional psychotherapy, wherever it develops, as a set of methods designed to resist all that is concentrationary. 'Concentrationary' is perhaps an old word — nowadays we speak of 'segregation'.

These structures of segregation exist everywhere, in a more or less veiled way. Any build-up of people, be it patients or children, in any place, develops, if one is not careful, oppressive structures simply by being in a group with an old-fashioned architectural and conceptual framework. *Institutional psychotherapy is perhaps the act of setting up all kinds of mechanisms to fight, every day, against all that could turn the whole of the 'collective' toward a concentrationary or segregationist structure.*

The problem of the mentally ill is still burdened by a lot of prejudices (despite the progress of Mental Hygiene, which tries to present the mentally ill in a more humane way). One has only to open a newspaper to see how the mentally ill are presented: as extremely dangerous people, as needing to be kept locked up. Yet, statistically, they are less dangerous than so-called normal people! Statistically, there is much more crime in so-called normal society. Yet newspaper headlines proclaim: 'The madman, who escaped from such an asylum, killed his mother-in-law, the police had to be called', and so on.

Also, even in the most modern healthcare structures, it is necessary to identify everything that can hinder the individuals from thriving within them: various elements developed out of this that later had to be theorized to maintain vigilance in the overall structure

I arrived at Saint-Alban's Hospital in 1947; I was an intern. The hospital had been 'humanized': cells had been abolished, and living spaces were acquired. At that time, in some other hospitals, the beds were adjoined: to get to your bed, you would have to climb over the beds of other patients; the only vital space was the dormitory corridor, there was no living room. People would stay there for years — they would meet at the foot of a staircase, or in the courtyard. So, the first thing to do is to organize a little bit of space, *a place where people can circulate a little bit more freely*.

But it's not just a question of letting them circulate 'freely' — because you quickly find that if no structure has been thought of, people start going round in circles, and it's a dead end. So, one has to create a place [*lieu*], but at the same time *devise occupations*, even the most rudimentary ones. The first effort of what was to become institutional psychotherapy was to tackle, in asylum structures, the most deprived areas; in particular, what are still called 'wards of agitated patients' [*quartiers des agités*] — there are also the 'wards of senile patients' [*quartiers des gâteux*].

It is now known that much of the senility [*gâtisme*] and agitation are actually effects, products of concentrationary life. One must have experienced it to see that agitated or senile people recover through the modification of their environment [*lieu*] and the activities they are given. The first major success of institutional psychotherapy involved modifying the wards for agitated patients, practically eliminating them.

When I came to this hospital, the wards of agitated patients had already ceased to exist. It was necessary to try to devise activities. This time saw the rise of active methods, especially in education. The reformatories were changing. There was a lot of talk about movements such as the C.E.M.É.A. (Centres d'entraînement aux méthodes d'éducation actives).[2]

Institutional psychotherapy always remained closely linked to these active education movements. This approach took psychiatric issues beyond the walls of the asylum, linking it to other fields, for example, summer camps, the I.M.P.,[3] and so on. All the doctors who later became part of this institutional psychotherapy movement did so in collaboration with the nurses. Training courses were organized to build awareness and know-how among the nurses (who had previously only been warders). In 1949, the first training course for psychiatric nurses took place as part of the C.E.M.É.A. on the initiative of various doctors (in particular Dr Le Guillant, Mrs Le Guillant, and Dr Daumézon).

---

2   Translators' note: Training Centres for Active Learning Methods. The C.E.M.É.A. were created during the Front Populaire period. They are a popular and modern education movement, and a training organization based on modern pedagogy principles and on the ideas of Célestin Freinet.

3   Translators' note: Institut médico-pédagogique (Medico-Pedagogical Institute).

These training courses took place several times a year, bringing together from fifty to one hundred nurses from all over France. In the long run, this led to a change, a raising of their critical awareness. The C.E.M.É.A. courses were something extraordinary. They lasted ten days. The nurses would come, for example, to a C.R.E.P.S.[4] Even if no particular technique was learned, the fact that people from about fifteen different hospitals would group together for ten days, the fact that each shared their own experiences in conversations, and that they understood that there were similar problems in hospitals other than their own, was enough to shake up habits. Some of them underwent something of a revelation, a crucial awareness that would change their lives. This does not mean that they could apply what they had learned! When they returned to their hospitals, they found themselves to be a minority that was bogged down in traditional structures — and sometimes this brought discouragement, depression. In the training courses, there were lectures, discussions, and learning of activity techniques — both group and ergotherapy.

Why am I recalling all of this? It may seem a little off topic. However, in talking about institutional psychotherapy, it seems to me important to think about all this, because we can do absolutely nothing in a hospital if we do not change something, not in the raw material of the architecture or the activities, but in the *consciousness* of the people who work there.

Now, this change does not happen in eight days, or in a year, or in ten years. It takes a very long time for nurses and doctors to become aware, and for that awareness to be *effective*. It should not be rushed. It's a bit like psychoanaly-

---

4   Translators' note: Centre de ressources, d'expertise et de performance sportive (Centre of Resources, Expertise and Sports Performance).

sis: you can't do psychoanalysis in eight days, it takes years
— it works, or it doesn't work. As far as training courses
are concerned, many have worked. But this has developed
a kind of collective intra-hospital resistance to colleagues
who went on these courses (even now, in some hospitals,
one hears reflections such as: 'You went on holiday, you're
going for a walk, you're a lazy bum, what does that mean,
training course?', etc.).

But institutional psychotherapy can develop only if
there is this progressive raising of awareness, attended by
all kinds of difficulties, even at the level of the nurses themselves. This has brought significant benefits. It was also
requested that the 'stewards', the 'heads of wards', 'administrators', and all the people who were involved in the status
of the establishments participate in these meetings. The
rigid structure of these establishments prevented the creation of places [*lieux*] where people could meet, talk, work.

This short introduction should not be forgotten, in
order to give sufficient weight to what can be said about institutional psychotherapy. Ten years ago, I certainly would
not have thought to mention all this. I might not have
talked about the C.E.M.É.A., or the concentration camps,
or the level of work of the nurses. But it's becoming a ne-
cessity, given everything that's been said and done under
this term. To situate the issue better, I will mention a
more localized experience: that of La Borde clinic in Cour-
Cheverny.

FROM SAINT-ALBAN TO LA BORDE

I started this psychiatric clinic in 1953. At that time, there
was no psychiatric hospital and practically no other clinics
in the Loir-et-Cher department. We had to absorb everything related to psychiatry in the department. One clinic

with only a hundred beds was absolutely inadequate: the situation was very difficult and unfavourable, but at the same time also a very privileged one. Given the position of the patients (who were mostly refused by hospitals in neighbouring departments, such as Loiret, Eure-et-Loir, Indre-et-Loire, etc., which were overcrowded), we were forced to manage as best we could to try to hospitalize as few as possible.

Not having many available places makes things interesting: you have to make some up, be inventive! To try to treat patients without hospitalizing them, or if they are hospitalized, to invent techniques for very short or very differentiated stays. Forced by events, we are quite simply obliged to do it. Of course, because it was myself and a few comrades who created this clinic, we had a certain freedom. We were not tied up in what is called the 'administrative straitjacket', although certain difficulties, perhaps more camouflaged, reappeared — such as the problem (which we could talk about later) of hierarchy, individual specializations, and so on.

We lived with the patients who came there. It was a kind of common group. This point seems a very important one to me since, without having thought about it, one of the major obstacles had been removed: segregation. In a hospital, segregation always exists. Think about the problem of admission. Admission has nothing to do with welcoming [*accueil*]; it's often even an unwelcoming [*anti-accueil*]. In some hospitals, admission was limited to registering a sick person's name and curriculum vitae, and then undressing them and putting them into uniform clothing: a technique of depersonalization. There was no admission of this sort at La Borde because from the outset we were a more or less familial group. So there were problems such as: What are we going to do with fifty or a hundred patients, nurses, and doctors? Of course, they have to be cured, that's what we're here for and they ought not to stay long: quite ordinary criteria… But what does it mean 'to care for' [*soigner*]? It was 1953, prior to the era of neuroleptics. You remember that, in France this era officially began with the introduction of Largactil around 1955. Institutional psychotherapy existed well before the era of neuroleptics.

Let's open a parenthesis to evoke again the wards of the agitated. Nowadays, when we talk about 'treating a ward of agitated patients', most people, most doctors, think of 'neuroleptics'. And the fact is that in many hospitals there is calm, sometimes even silence. But you have to check the doses — as if treatment of the agitated consisted solely in sprinkling them with all kinds of neuroleptics!

I'm not saying that institutional psychotherapy is against neuroleptics, quite the contrary — we even aim to develop quite original methods of prescription (both qualitative and quantitative). But taking care of people is not just about giving them medication. Even in ordinary medicine, this is clear: you don't have to be a psychiatrist to see that treating pneumonia requires a minimum of contact. Even the most physical of treatments work more or less well depending on the contact you have with the family and the patient. You have to be somewhat friendly to the people you are treating…

Thus, we asked ourselves the following question: 'What can we do with the people here, apart from giving them medication, apart from giving them treatments such as insulin therapy, electroshock therapy, and so on?' 'Leave them in peace, we ought not to bother them.' The intention is often good. However, if you limit yourself to saying, 'Don't bother them', then they will quickly bother you. Because when a patient is delusional, or schizophrenic, or confused, or melancholic, you can't just say 'Don't bother them', otherwise incidents will occur, and you'll be forced to intervene. And if you don't think ahead, then in some weeks or months you will have to resort to the most oppressive structures (to prevent someone from committing suicide, for example).

One of the axioms we devised, then, was the following; that in whatever place [*lieu*] we are living for a certain period of time, a *maximum possibility of circulation* must be created. This axiom is often unrecognized in many modern architectural designs. When an official text states that a hospital 'with three hundred beds' should be built, can we be happy with this formulation? In surgery, this is expected, resting areas must be set up; but in psychiatry people do not stay in their beds! When someone stays in bed, one even starts to worry: staying in bed creates extraordinary isolation.

We ought therefore to insist on the need for social spaces! We are trying to introduce this axiom into architectural standards, together with teams of architects who are now familiar with institutional psychotherapy. The necessary number of square metres of surface area must be calculated and the necessary diversity of places planned… But this only makes sense if the patients are able to go to them! There are, we know, very good, very clean hospitals, with beautiful lawns, but where there is no live circulation: there are libraries, but one is not allowed to go in them, for example. We therefore have to *create places where people can go.*

This is the sense of the axiom of 'freedom of circulation'. But what does this mean in practice? There are basic facilities: a kitchen, administrative offices, a pharmacy, a library, a theatre, and so on. When we say 'freedom of circulation', we see barriers and resistances emerge. I often use the most caricatured example of what happens at the level of the kitchen. There were dramas — many of the cooks did not cope. 'Freedom of circulation' means that patients can go to the kitchen, take care of it, and talk to the head cook. When the head cook is not prepared, hasn't done training at the C.E.M.É.A., comes simply to do the job of cooking, and then is sent 'crazy people' to... well, the cook will cry: 'They will touch the knobs, the gas, they will spill the soup on me...' The first tendency is to barricade oneself. It's normal for people to erect barricades: to close the door, to install a counter to pass dishes through, and then say 'leave me alone, I can't work', and so on. All this is for the cook.

Patients also go to the administrative office to see the guy doing the accounts, or to the pharmacy to shout at the person counting the pills. This can and does indeed create a lot of conflicts. But what is interesting, in this milieu of free circulation, is precisely the possibility of creating conflicts — not in order to annoy people, but to create life; for, without conflicts, there is no life. It's not a question of acting in a perverse way; but as soon as there is conflict, we have to take it as an occasion to try to talk about it to make relationships that are better adapted. It started out in a very simple way. We say, 'We have to let them circulate', and straightaway we notice that there is resistance. If we give in, the cook will barricade himself in the kitchen: it will snowball, and we will quickly return to the concentrationary system, the patients will have to be locked up in their rooms... We won't need to talk any longer about 'social square metres'! At the end of the day, there will be a regression.

Once we're committed, there's no going back. I remember a more or less heroic time: we had created what we called 'traps', for the cook, for example. For the cook or for people who could not stand the intrusion of the patients into their territory. We devised something we saw as essential to adding a little bit of life to the collectivity: a sort of bar, a counter, where drinks, sweets, cakes, and tobacco were sold under the responsibility of a small group of patients. We knew that the cook would go to the bistro of the neighbouring village to play billiards or buy tobacco. We said to ourselves: 'If he has to go to the bar to buy his tobacco, it will force him to get to know the patients and not be afraid of them.' He found he was obliged to go there; we invited him to evening gatherings, to theatre and dance sessions, etc. Overcoming, eliminating fear, and dispelling this prejudice held by the layperson to enable him or her to enter into contact with the patients and accept this basic principle: freedom of circulation. Over time, this was achieved; now, it works very well… But many cooks quit!

As a result, people who work there, but who don't have an official position as a 'counsellor' [*moniteur*] or 'nurse', find themselves absorbed in a *relation* with the patient whether they like it or not, and how they respond may be of therapeutic importance. This point can be further elaborated upon by stating that *any function of any person working in a psychiatric centre is always indexed to a psychotherapeutic coefficient*. What we call the therapeutic coefficient, or rather the 'psychotherapeutic coefficient' in the broadest sense of the term, takes on a clearer meaning when we think that the way we greet a paranoid person can completely change the ambience of the day. If the counsellor, or cook, or secretary, talks to the patient in a normal way, it can change from top to bottom the person who feels persecuted, who is picking fights with everybody… It may be the cook who talks to him, the cook being neither doctor, counsellor, educator nor nurse. This factor is sometimes decisive on the psychotherapeutic level, of infinitely greater importance than all the consultations that the patient may have in the doctor's office. It's hard to admit.

Simply sending the cook to the C.E.M.É.A. training course is not enough; there is a certain limit to these C.E.M.É.A. courses, because they are external to the establishment. You have to work the milieu, work on something that is there, on site, a kind of useless network that keeps breaking down. What I say as regards the cook, of course, has the same value for the rest of the staff. I'm thinking, for example, of cleaning ladies. I have often been criticized because when I was asked, 'Who does psychotherapy in your establishment?' in a somewhat provocative way, I answered, 'The cleaning ladies'. Group psychotherapists, in general, did not like that.

It's a good thing that there are no (or almost no) cleaning ladies anymore, so everyone has to do the cleaning. Cleaning is a noble activity. To clean a multi-bed room, you would have to be an exceptional psychotherapist to be able to talk to the people who are there, who are lying in bed. Saying to this or that patient: 'Here, we've come to make your bed' — it's not about just throwing him out of the bed! You have to be able to talk to him and say, 'Did you sleep well? What are you going to do today? Do you have to glue some paper back on there?' Or: 'We should go to the city, buy bedside lamps!' Doing the housework, which is to say, creating an ordinary everyday ambience. This does not go well with the usual standards of psychotherapy, but we have to work with what is there and this is what we have. Now, this is what there is, to be able to shape it, there are people there who are not trained, who have not obtained diplomas, but who are there all the same, and who have, whether they like it or not, a positive or negative impact on such and such a patient.

If we had the time to do a very detailed report on a patient from the day they were admitted to the hospital until their discharge, we would ask ourselves what played a role in their progression: was it because the doctor saw them so many times a week, was it because of this or that medication? Of course, all of this is important. But it may be that it was a conversation that this person had with their roommate or with the cleaning lady, or with whomever, on a certain day, at a certain moment of anxiety. It is elements like these, which might not be remembered, that matter immensely in practice. How can we turn it into an advantage?

That's when I realized that there is a bare minimum that has to be done, and this bare minimum is often very demanding: a minimum of briefings, as well as a minimum of training sessions with a very heterogeneous staff including doctors, cleaning ladies, cooks, educators, nurses, psychologists. These meetings only make sense if they are repeated; if there is a certain ritual that is part of the work. However, we know very well that, in all establishments, when people say, 'We're going to have a meeting', many people answer back, 'Another waste of time! We don't have time to clean up, or to work, or to give shots as it is!'... It's true, meetings are often an extraordinary waste of time... Because they are badly done! But we realize that by having these meetings, at ground level, by saying: 'What are we doing today? You saw such and such patient, what did he say? How was he? What did it make you think of?'; we can make use of all the exchanges that can happen in a meeting, provided there are no hierarchical barriers.

It is necessary to break down hierarchical barriers so people can express themselves; we then realize that we can save an extraordinary amount of time because the patients, who until then had remained completely passive, say things like: 'We're here to be cared for, not to work, we're here to have our breakfast served to us in bed....'. All these arguments quickly disappear, so that we see that, based on discussions in meetings, we can create activity groups in which the patients themselves take everything in hand. We then see that among all these patients, there are people who are much more qualified than the psychologists, nurses, and so on, people who are simply asleep and just need to be woken up. These are people who one crushes if one confines them in traditional structures. They will wake up, and, at that moment, the staff (what we call the staff, meaning those who do not have the status of patients) will be able to have a slightly different function. Instead of being busy with tasks, instead of being physical staff, they will become staff who are able to think a little, they will have time to think, to organize things.

It's not a question either of going to extremes, of saying things like 'Oh, I don't work anymore, I observe, and I'm a psycho-sociologist!' That's a risk! The patients do the cleaning, and we come to see from time to time, once in the morning: 'How is it going?' That is not what it is about at all: you have to stay involved because otherwise it would have been better to do nothing. The risk of this kind of technique shifting is extremely common. For, without realizing it, you return to what goes on in regular asylums: there are the good workers. 'The good workers', you know what the good workers are. There is the ward for agitated patients, the ward for senile patients, the ward for I don't know what, and then there are the good workers. In a large asylum, there are many good workers; they do a peculiar kind of work, to the extent that if we removed the good workers, the hospital's finances would suffer greatly!

This work is very important: agricultural work, masonry, furniture making, which doesn't cost much... So, the goal is not to fall into that trap. It is tricky, it is difficult. It is certain that if the people who are there do the work, even with the counsellors, the work will be effective. This problem must be honestly addressed. These people are hospitalized; there is no employment contract with them, and here they are working, cooking with the chefs. They can very well say, 'This is exploitation!' It is true, it is exploitation if we keep that perspective. And if we start paying them....

But we cannot pay them; we can't give someone who is hospitalized a salary. If they are paid a low wage, it will be said to be shameful! A somewhat proud person will say, 'Keep your money, I don't want to be paid a low wage for work as qualified as that of your counsellor, if not more.'

This is therefore another source of conflicts, but these conflicts are very interesting because they call into question something much deeper: the very status of the people who are there, but also their status when they were outside, when they were not ill. What did you do before — were you a cook, a driver, or did you work in a factory? So all of this will be questioned, and we will have to say we can't pay you, but still, there is something to do. We must not fall into this hypocrisy: 'Oh, but you are doing occupational therapy! It is healing you! You should even pay us to do this cooking or cleaning work in our place'... We can't go that far.

Obviously, in society as it is, there are contradictions; it is not easy. It is better to be occupied than to do nothing. It's true, it's true that by doing nothing, you become ill; you need to be occupied, but it's not mandatory. But there's everything in there, among the staff, and there are guys who still take advantage of the 'good patients'. For example, women who like to knit, make knits, skirts, whatever. They do it on the sly, like that, to such and such a counsellor, for example a thousand-Franc note is given for something one would buy for twenty thousand. We have to watch out for that.

That's when we realize that *we can't do anything if, conjointly, we don't create a real internal society composed essentially of the patients themselves, a society which will manage itself.* This is, in my opinion, a second axiom: in collective living, it is always very harmful to live piled up. We cannot say it is not human, because it is as human as anything else, but living in a crowd creates toxins and conflicts that are sometimes entirely negative. Therefore, we must find a way to resist this. How do we solve, for example, this little problem of salary, of allowances, as it is called elsewhere?

It is not easy to create a society of patients within the hospital and for this society to manage itself, to be autonomous, because the patients are not going to create it themselves: it has to come from a certain framing or supervision [*encadrement*], from the team that is there, from the doctor. But if we do it directly, by bringing together all the patients who are willing to come and listen one fine day, and by saying: 'My friends, we are going to create a society, and you will be the ones running it, you will do parties, workshops, etc.', if we leave it there, it would have been better not to do anything at all, because very quickly that creates an extraordinarily corrupting ambience: indeed, we create a system of framing relations between the administration and the patients of a kind that is correctly called *paternalistic*. Now, you know that the paternalistic relationship is something very dangerous, something more or less reducible to: 'We're going to please daddy'.... The medical director is pleased that we get together, and then we have a bar, and we have a celebration every eight days, that we have a library, and so forth. We have to find something else. So, it seems that the cleverest thing that has been found so far is the creation within the establishments of what was first called The Club, the therapeutic club. *The therapeutic club only makes sense if it is not connected directly to the doctor's demand or desire, it must have an autonomous existence, independent of any system of exploitation.*

Indeed, whether it is a clinic or a hospital, we are talking about a commercial undertaking: budget management and operational efficiency are necessary. How do you escape this pressure of exploitation? To try to solve this problem, societies have been set up that are part of one establishment, but depend on another organism. The most widespread or common ones right now are the Croix-Marine societies. Some people have heard of the Fédération des sociétés de Croix-Marine, a federation of Mental Hygiene societies that started in Saint-Alban in 1947, the centre of which was established in Clermont-Ferrand.

The purpose of these societies was initially to take over the work of doing 'good deeds' — it was part of charitable work, but it was to structure it better. In other words, 'What are we going to do with the poor patient who is leaving the hospital? We have to find him a job, a family placement.'... But quickly, we said: 'It's all very well to take care of people when they get out, when it happens that they do leave, but we should be able to get them out; we should therefore provide Mental Hygiene not only outside the asylums, but also inside.' There was, in fact, a paradox: Mental Hygiene was done outside the asylums, but the concentrationary structures were being preserved on the inside. So we had to try to do Mental Hygiene work on the inside.

This work faced many difficulties and resistances. During a general assembly of the Croix-Marine societies in 1953, a Spanish-born doctor at Saint-Alban at that time, François Tosquelles, officially advocated for the creation of what he called 'Hospital Committees' within hospitals.

These Hospital Committees have developed just about everywhere. But there are pitfalls here too. For example, a ministerial circular of February 1958 recommends that, in the organization within hospitals of sociotherapy, ergotherapy, and so on, Croix-Marine Hospital Committees be created. A Hospital Committee, because it is affiliated with the Croix-Marine Federation, does not depend at all on the hospital; its management is handled by the patients themselves through a democratic system of election — president, secretary, and so on. Nurses and hospital staff also participate in these committees; it is recommended to have nurses, to have administrators. They can help, but they should not have the majority.

For this to work, the Committee must therefore make a *contract,* a very specific contract, with the establishment. This contract can provide, for example, that the establishment cedes to the association (they are associations under the law of 1901, so they can make donations) this or that area of the establishment itself: a playground, a number of rooms, spaces to do workshops, and so on. But the important thing, which is often not respected, is that these Hospital Committees are able to take over the work of ergotherapy... That may seem like a small detail, but it is crucial — otherwise, it's a sleight of hand: they will say they've set up a Hospital Committee, but it's not true....

Indeed, by taking charge of all the hospital's ergotherapy, all the non-productive and productive workshops (carpentry, raphiatherapy,[5] etc.), we meet areas of conflict, bringing a certain 'ferment' into the hospital. In just a few years, the Hospital Committee went from having a small budget, i.e. a packet of cigarettes, given to the 'good

---

5   Translators' note: Oury probably refers to a therapy based on weaving of raffia palm.

workers' each month, to managing considerable sums. I remember that in 1947, the administration paid 8,000 francs a year for all the entertainment in a hospital with six hundred patients. And out of these 8,000 francs, 4,000 francs were needed to pay for a flag on 14 July. With the remaining 4,000 francs, we had to buy presents for Christmas — that was all we could do.

Well, ten or so years ago, the Hospital Committee raised 15 to 20 million [francs] a year — which is not bad! But it's easy to see where resistance can come from. When an entire administrative structure traditionally operates with workshops that are performance-based, it's clear that there has been some sabotage, and it's understandable that this Hospital Committee structure is not an easy thing to accept.

So, the contract had to be better elaborated. For example, it was important to acknowledge that in the accounting plan that donations were made to the hospital around 1956–57, specifically the figures related to ergotherapy could be managed by the Hospital Committee. Therefore, the Committee could officially manage the workshops, under the control of the administration.

It may be a little tedious to go over all this, but it is so important that I will do it anyway. Ignoring this connection risks degrading the undertaking, despite its advocates' good intentions. For example, in some modern hospitals we are seeing attempts at implementing institutional psychotherapy. Workshops are created, then a Club. Architects are building what have been called Social Centres. I find it better not to talk about it. I'm thinking of a hospital that has a social centre that costs half a billion ... It's not bad. It's extraordinary, it's beautiful! But the patients don't go there. The people from the city are the ones who go there, famous people and others. This makes for a mixing of the population, but it does not tally with anything; and what could we have done with half a billion… How many little Christmas presents could we have gotten with such a sum? In a word, this is a kind of degeneration of the spirit of the Hospital Committee.

And often today, when we talk to doctors, to interns, about the urgent need to create Croix-Marine style Hospital Committees, everyone laughs. They say 'the Croix-Marine, but what is the Croix-Marine?' So one doesn't dare talk about it any further. But all the same we must try to save it.

But I was getting to the point about the various conflicts that result from institutional reshuffle. *These conflicts can only be resolved if we set up an internal structure in the establishment that is constituted in a wholly different way to the structure of the establishment itself.* Most of the time, an establishment structure is vertical, let's say pyramidal: the director, the bursar, the warder, and so on, the doctor, and then at the bottom of the ladder, the good workers. It's very difficult to tackle such a structure directly, but, *if it is accepted that it is possible to create another structure, one that is not vertical but horizontal, and that does not have a sort of rigid axis, but will have many small axes, a structure I call polycentric* (centred on a secretariat, a general assembly, workshops, etc., so that people are able to take on responsibility) *we will find ourselves faced with the need to invent* workshops of all kinds, which may stay for a long time or which may disappear — that is, to invent *something very mobile, able to adapt to the demands of the patients who are there.*

We can't envisage anything when we're stuck in pyramid-like structures, not even with the best of intentions. On the other hand, the polycentric structure is the instrument for setting up a whole where opportunities for exchanges and encounters can be multiplied, and systems of conflict can be settled. For example, at any given time, how can we respond to the demand for payment that seemed legitimate to some patients who were doing a job? 'We can't, because that would be hypocritical, we can't pay you a salary'? To pay someone and not have it be a salary, this always leaves things open to interpretation… On the other hand, we can estimate, despite accounting complications, the amount of work that all the patients carry out. It can be estimated quickly by substitution, by saying as follows: 'We would have to hire this many staff to do this; deducting Social Security costs, tax returns, etc., we can pay this sum to the Club and the Hospital Committee as a whole, which will become the Hospital Committee's treasury, fed by a collective effort.' The distribution of the money will be done in a completely different way than the individual payment of remuneration.

It's important to remember that people are there to be treated, to try to find a solution to their problems. We can thus try to set up a commission made up, for example, of nurses, doctors, and patients, for considering each case. For example, a guy has to get out, but he has no family, no job, no housing… It's a very common occurrence. We can rely on structures that we develop jointly, structures ranging from the Croix-Marine to the social service office in the town, sheltered workshops, etc. But these are only provisional measures, and they are quickly swamped. It can happen that someone needs to live for fifteen days outside to try their luck. The Hospital Committee, through this commission, can decide: 'We're going to give him or her 50,000 francs.' 'Go ahead, and in two weeks, come back and tell us what you've done.' With these 50,000 francs, he must be able to find a place to live, food, and work. Often it works, and sometimes it doesn't.

Everyone accepts that this is a kind of solidarity fund, but the main advantage is that this solidarity fund is managed by the very group of people who are there, who know each other. This eliminates the somewhat dubious kind of charity that reappears every time someone says: 'We will help you'. The guy leaves in a much more reassured way, he knows that the money is being given to him by friends. They can also say to him: 'Just pay us back when you have the money' — depending on the case. But then the person feels far more connected when they make a commitment to their fellow human beings rather than if it's made through the administration. That's one of the advantages of Hospital Committees. But these Hospital Committee funds can also be used for a film club, such as to buy a device that improves the way of life inside the hospital, without it coming directly from the establishment management.

Why did I insist on these few examples? To try to introduce a difficult question, one underlying this formulation: *institutional psychotherapy is the act of setting up techniques of mediation.* 'Mediation' is not a felicitous choice of word, but it is the one used. It seems that the Hospital Committee is a solid example in which mediation is established between relationships that can develop from person to person, or from a collective to a person. These are direct relationships that, whether we like it or not, are often quite oppressive, permeated with prejudices. The intervention of a doctor, if only because of their role, their status, their place in society, will always be affected by a certain distortion.

We can see that we have to try to introduce something, another structure — what we call a 'structure of mediation'. If the Hospital Committee is one of them, we must not forget that it is in everyday life, on a daily basis, that we must introduce structures of mediation. You meet someone, you don't really know what to say, you offer them a cigarette. We can say that cigarettes are a form of mediation that make engaging in dialogue possible. When we say that, in order to be able to work in a collective and to create a milieu of free circulation in which people can talk better with each other, a bar is required where newspapers and tobacco are sold, because it's true that the exchange will take place there, on the occasion of someone buying something. Even people not expecting it will find themselves caught in a certain 'relationship trap', because they came to buy something; they will engage in a minimum of dialogue, which can sometimes be of extraordinary importance. That's when people recognize each other: they knew each other well before they were hospitalized, they'll reunite there, a conversation will spark, they'll go for a walk together, and perhaps the other person he has met will find him a job, perhaps simply by saying, 'Look, I have connections, my family has a ....'. This, we can see, involves the creation of a system of mediation — but it is true also in the activities of theatre, cinema, newspapers, and so on. *It is not enough to say that something must be set up that is able to create an exchange. It is all well and good to make exchanges, but ultimately it is necessary to have some mediating structure* ['un support'], *and above all an occasion.*

If you would like, perhaps we could talk a bit, and pick up on this problem later. I've presented things more or less roughly, but a more theoretical explanation of this problematic would need to be tackled, which would enable us to see that the psychiatric example can very well be applied to other structures. I am thinking in particular of schools, active education methods and then the I.M.P., and so on. But I think that it is preferable to use what I have just said, as a form of mediation, as it were in order to engage in a dialogue.

QUESTIONS AND ANSWERS

[Audience]: *There's a question I'm asking myself regarding institutional psychotherapy: I have the impression that I.P. [institutional psychotherapy] is tolerated by the country in which we live, at least within the political structures that we have at present. Because one of two things is true: either establishments that operate on the basis of institutional psychotherapy constitute a new form of segregation, or they run the risk of creating a new form of segregation, insofar as they are organized around themselves, but where the exchanges are perhaps organized within the establishment. This constitutes progress, because it didn't exist before; but what is exchanged with the outside? And doesn't the establishment then appear, in the eyes of the outside world, as a collectivity of the mad?*

Jean Oury: Presenting institutional psychotherapy in a very fragmented way, as I have done in this introduction, may lend itself to your criticism and make you think that, indeed, there is some kind of rather closed world being established, with a particular structure. We've also been accused of creating an intra-asylum neo-society; but this seems to be a misunderstanding. It was to avoid this that I insisted on pointing out (perhaps too quickly) something that seemed fundamental: that we were obliged, given the overload and growing demand for hospitalization, to find a way to heal as quickly as possible. It was, as it were, a guarantee that there would be no 'confinement', to use Foucault's term; it was to create an anti-confinement [*anti-renfermerie*].

This 'anti-confinement' dimension was totally guaranteed, because some people had to leave for others to enter!

It was also a guarantee against the formation of an enclosed universe, because it's simply a matter of letting some people in and pushing others out, without bothering with them anymore. Moreover, the tragedy with all these psychiatric problems is that when you take on someone who is ill, you take them on for life. You can't treat it like appendicitis or the flu. For example, there are people I came to know twenty years ago, I did not see them for two years, and then here they are again. For example, with the recent flu epidemics, we've seen an upsurge in asthenia, fatigue, and depression. People I hadn't seen in ten years came back with acute, suicidal depression, requiring urgent treatment. They'd been fine for ten years, but then they'd come back. I didn't even have to reacquaint myself with them, I recognized them. I had their file card, I knew their family, and so on. It was a kind of continuity.

This is to tell you that the hospital, the clinic, such as I presented it, is a kind of hub where people come back easily; but that doesn't mean they can't leave it! They are obliged to leave it, but precautions must be taken in order to let them go: you can't throw someone in the water; you have to follow their progress, make them come back... What is created from the fact that the experiment works, even if someone came for fifteen days, is the equivalent of what happens in the C.E.M.É.A. courses for nurses: a revelation. People who are in their little lives — go to the office in the morning, come home at night, 'we only have illnesses of the body'... It's easy to see how far these prejudices go. For example, traditionally trained nurses have a lot of difficulty adapting to this work. If you tell such a nurse, 'Enough with the injections, you need to go run a gardening or cooking workshop', it's an affront! 'What, me, a qualified nurse, you want me to dig or wash dishes? It cannot be!' Similarly (and this has become famous), when a psychologist arrived at La Borde clinic, I would say to them: 'Do the dishes. A month of washing up!'. When you're a real psychologist, washing up is a fantastic job for observing; you can make extraordinary observations in such places.

I give these few examples to illustrate how we fight against this 'dualistic prejudice'. On the other hand, if the Hospital Committee is misunderstood, it will close in on itself — and it's to avoid this enclosure that what we called 'fairs' are organized. But fairs can also remain an activity of patronage, of good deeds: the poor sick people who are there, gathering funds, having fun... the 'tender charity' of fairs!

To avoid this, we organized open-air fairs, which became major events throughout the region. I remember, for example, that two or three years ago, this Hospital Committee organized what we called 'culture month' — which, by the way, went on for two months. That year's theme was 'La Sologne' (the clinic being located in the Sologne region). It was extraordinary! The patients themselves organized, for example, along with the enthusiastic help of the local population, evening gatherings in the villages, several a week; people volunteered both for folk-lore activities, and to organize conferences with historians, geographers, archaeologists, novelists, filmmakers, etc. All segments of the population were interested. At another fair, something extraordinary was organized by the Hospital Committee: all evening the Republican Guard played Vivaldi and Mozart at the Blois Cathedral... All that is to say that it's not at all 'confined'; it's well known that people circulate, and families often come on Sundays to spend a day there. So we need to open up these structures to the 'outside world'. Otherwise we remain in a chapel, in isolation...

Everything that's closed off becomes dangerous: it ferments! And whether we are talking about communist ideas or something else, the fact that they're inside a closed structure means what occurs is something other than communism, an idealism of who knows what sort — but it has nothing to do with communism, even if the money is shared. Besides, it's not about sharing the money. The people who are there are on Social Security; it's not the Club that feeds them.

Isn't the desire to live afterwards precisely… Maybe not exactly in the same way, because at the time they were ill, and in principle they got better… But isn't the desire to live afterwards precisely in that way, somewhere else?

I understand the question well; it's often asked. Never (despite having seen thousands of people over time…), never has it come up. It only comes up when it's asked! As in any hospital, there's what we call 'sedimentation' (which is a bit of a geological term), and 'chronicity'.

We can say that the chronically ill are not those who stay. The chronically ill can often work, stay at home, helped by psychotherapy, pharmacology… These techniques enable us to act with extraordinary flexibility, to discharge as many patients as possible, or to not even hospitalize them at all. By contrast, there is a category of patients we call the 'sediment'. This sediment is composed of patients who may be severely schizophrenic, but above all by patients whose social conditions are unsatisfactory. They are rejected, forgotten, even if they have friendly visits from time to time. These are people who are forgotten, and for whom nothing can be done in terms of the society as it currently stands — except when we are lucky enough to find a few family placements. We can't use this layer of sedimentation as an excuse to say that they like staying there! Other patients just want to get out and work.

The problem you ask is the famous 'sector' problem, which is far from being solved. I don't think we can solve the problem of the sector by not wanting to see it, by turning a blind eye to the need for a specific living centre (at least at certain stages of mental illness) to treat people.

The sector is:

- Make this centre as open as possible, so that there is two-way circulation, so that people can come in, and so that patients can go out to take on responsibilities elsewhere.

- But at the same time, it means creating, for example, what I mentioned earlier: a social office in the neighbouring town, where people can look for work, housing, to have meeting places, small units — not necessarily of 'aftercare', as they say, but units that could just as easily be called 'pre-care', which often prevent hospitalization.

- It also means collaborating with schools; for example, we can link the work of dispensaries with the problem of special classes. In other words, [the educational and pedagogical work] has, at a certain level, the same theoretical aim of taking up what is at issue in mental illness: we can say that mental illness is an illness of relationality — that's very approximate. On the other hand, we can affirm that the institution, in the end, is everywhere. The first institution that exists in today's society, the institution that teaches you to talk and walk, is the family. You can't do institutional psychiatry without constant contact with the family, without 'working' the family milieu.

I don't know if I've answered exactly what you were asking?

It always depends on this question of 'tolerance', because this problem arises in psychiatry, but it also arises in maladjusted childhood. In my opinion, perhaps because I'm a psychiatrist, these problems are identical. A so-called 're-education' centre, in fact, has the same problems as a psychiatric service, as a psychiatric hospital. And I have to say, moreover, that educators sensed some of the pitfalls long before psychiatrists, and avoided some of them; there are others they didn't avoid, but all the same, whether it's psychiatry or maladjusted childhood, the big question for me is: 'How will a society like ours be able to tolerate for long such structures that bubble up, that try to ask questions, that try to understand and that try, in fact, to get people out a bit, as you were saying, of the TV, of the little car, of this or that?'

This certainly creates problems… But it's a more general question than that of psychiatry itself: we have to choose between what we might call a 'hyper-segregationist' universe, which is unfortunately becoming more and more pronounced — a whole system of compartmentalization, to lock up the mad or children.

You know, what I'm saying here, I could also say about high schools — but I won't, because that would be too violent. We can talk about hospitals, because they're still, let's say, an almost sacred domain: the mad, the mentally ill, we can talk about them. At a certain point, you could even do anything inside, even engage in total communism — no one cared at all: as long as it stayed in the asylum! They even said: 'You see, it's good for the insane, but not for the others…'. But there's no doubt that there can be a danger here: all these currents of institutional psychotherapy presenting themselves as subversive, risk triggering such a *reaction* that the practice of institutional psychotherapy will be barred. To avoid this kind of 'reaction', I find it very beneficial to take advantage of existing official structures, such as those of the Croix-Marine societies: it is a guarantee after all.

TRANSLATED BY ANTHONY FARAMELLI
AND MARLON MIGUEL

References

Ajzenberg, Armand, *L'Abandon à la mort... de 76000 fous par le régime de Vichy* and André Castelli, *Un hôpital psychiatrique sous Vichy (1940–1945)* (Paris: L'Harmattan, 2012)

Apprill, Olivier, 'Tosquelles et la psychiatrie concrète', in *François Tosquelles et le travail*, ed. by Pascale Molinier (Paris: Éditions d'une, 2018), pp. 159–80

Artaud, Antonin, 'Alienation and Black Magic', in *Artaud the Mômo*, ed. by Stephen Barber and trans. by Clayton Eshleman (Zurich/Berlin: Diaphanes, 2020), pp. 88–111

Audier, Serge, *La Pensée anti-68. Essai sur les origines d'une restauration intellectuelle* (Paris: La Découverte, 2008) <https://doi.org/10.3917/dec.audie.2009.01>

Balvet, Paul, 'De l'autonomie de la profession psychiatrique', in *Au-delà de l'asile d'aliénés et de l'hôpital psychiatrique*, Documents de *L'Information psychiatrique* (Paris: Desclée de Brouwer, 1946), pp. 11–18

Bernard, Claude, *Introduction à l'étude de la médecine expérimentale* [1865] (Paris: Flammarion, 2008)

Blondel, Charles, 'Quelques réflexions sur la schizophrénie', *Travaux de la clinique psychiatrique de la faculté de Médecine de Strasbourg*, 9 (1931), pp. 7–42

Bonhoeffer, Karl, 'Die exogenen Reaktionstypen', *Archiv für Psychiatrie und Nervenkrankheiten*, 58 (1917), pp. 58–70 <https://doi.org/10.1007/BF02036408>

Bonnafé, Lucien, 'Interprétation du fait psychiatrique selon la méthode historique de K. Marx et F. Engels', *L'Évolution psychiatrique*, [13].4 (1948), pp. 75–105

—— 'Le Personnage du psychiatre', *L'Évolution psychiatrique*, 13.3 (1948), pp. 23–56

Bonnafé, Lucien, and Georges Daumézon, 'L'Internement, conduite primitive de la société devant la maladie mentale: recherche d'une attitude plus évoluée', in *Le Malade mental dans la société*, Documents de *L'Information psychiatrique* (Paris: Desclée de Brouwer, 1946), pp. 79–107

Bonnafé, Lucien, and Sven Follin, 'À propos de la psychogenèse: étude critique de l'organo-dynamisme de Henri Ey: les bases d'une psychiatrie concrète, science originale de l'homme-psychopathe', in *Le Problème de la psychogenèse des névroses et des psychoses*, ed. by Henri Ey (Paris: Desclée de Brouwer, 1950; repr. Paris: Tchou, 2004)

Bonnafé, Lucien, and others, 'Note sur l'originalité du pathologique d'après la psychanalyse et sur la valeur du complexe comme perspective structurale dans l'existence pathologique', *Annales médico-psychologiques*, 104.2 (1946), pp. 58–63

—— 'Valeur de la théorie de la forme en psychiatrie: la dialectique du moi et du monde et l'événement morbide', *Annales médico-psychologiques*, 103.2 (1945), pp. 279–84

Bueltzingsloewen, Isabelle von, *L'Hécatombe des fous. La Famine dans les hôpitaux psychiatriques français sous l'Occupation* (Paris: Flammarion, 2009)

Caló, Susana, 'The Grid', *Anthropocene Curriculum*, 23 April 2016 <https://www.anthropocene-curriculum.org/contribution/the-grid> [accessed 7 April 2024]

Caló, Susana, and Godofredo Pereira, 'CERFI: Militant Analysis, Collective Equipment and Institutional Programming', *Royal Collect of Art* <https://www.rca.ac.uk/research-innovation/projects/cerfi-militant-analysis-collective-equipment-and-institutional-programming/> [accessed 7 April 2024]

Canguilhem, Georges, *The Normal and the Pathological* (New York: Zone Books, 1991)

Castel, Robert, *La Gestion des risques* (Paris: Les Éditions de Minuit, 2011)

Coffin, Jean-Christophe, 'Un syndicat en psychiatrie: une association d'intérêt?', in *Syndicats et associations: concurrence ou complémentarité?*, ed. by Danielle Tartakowsky and Françoise Tétard (Rennes: Presses universitaires de Rennes, 2015), pp. 139–47 <https://doi.org/10.4000/books.pur.25327>

Comte, Auguste, *Cours de philosophie positive* [1830] (Paris: Hermann, 1998)

Daumézon, Georges, 'La Protection de la santé mentale en France. État actuel et projets de rénovation', in *Le Malade mental dans la société*, Documents de *L'Information psychia-trique* (Paris: Desclée de Brouwer, 1946), pp. 9–77

Daumézon, Georges, and Philippe Koechlin, 'La Psychothéra-pie institutionnelle française contemporaine', *Anais portu-gueses de psiquiatria*, 4.4 (1952), pp. 271–312

De Brito, Carlos, 'Jacques Postel, de loin et de près, *in memoriam*', *L'Information psychiatrique*, 99.2 (2023)

Dublineau, Jean, and Sven Follin, 'Examen clinique d'un "bour-reau domestique". Rôle des interactions conjugales', *An-nales médico-psychologiques*, 100.1 (1942), pp. 326–29

Eribon, Didier, *Michel Foucault*, trans. by Betsy Wing (Cam-bridge, MA: Harvard University Press, 1991)

Ey, Henri, ed., *Le Problème de la psychogenèse des névroses et des psychoses* (Paris: Desclée de Brouwer, 1950; repr. Paris: Tchou, 2004)

Ey, Henri, Julián de Ajuriaguerra, and Henry Hécaen, eds, *Les Rapports de la neurologie et de la psychiatrie* (Paris: Her-mann, 1947)

Fanon, Frantz, *Black Skin, White Masks*, trans. by Charles Lam Markmann (London: Pluto Press, 1986)

Fanon, Frantz, and François Tosquelles, 'On Some Cases Treated with the Bini Method', in Frantz Fanon, *Alien-ation and Freedom*, ed. by Jean Khalfa and Robert J. C. Young, and trans. by Steven Corcoran (London: Blooms-bury, 2018), pp. 285–90

Fanon, Frantz, and Jacques Azoulay, 'Social Therapy in a Ward of Muslim Men: Methodological Difficulties', in Fanon, *Alien-ation and Freedom*, ed. by Jean Khalfa and Robert J. C. Young, and trans. by Steven Corcoran (London: Blooms-bury, 2018), pp. 353–71

Fay, Margaret, 'The 1844 Economic and Philosophic Manu-scripts of Karl Marx: A Critical Commentary and Interpret-ation' (unpublished doctoral thesis, University of Califor-nia, Berkeley, 1979)

Follin, Sven, 'Rationalisme moderne et psychiatrie', *L'Évolution psychiatrique*, [13].4 (1948)

Goldstein, Kurt, *The Organism: A Holistic Approach to Biology Derived from Pathological Data in Man* (New York: Zone Books, 1995)

Guattari, Félix, 'La Borde: A Clinic Unlike Any Other', in *Chaoso-phy: Texts and Interviews 1972–1977*, ed. by Sylvère Lotringer, and trans. by David L. Sweet, Jarred Becker, and Taylor Adkins (Los Angeles: Semiotext(e), 2009), pp. 176–94

—— *Psychanalyse et transversalité. Essais d'analyse institutionnelle* (Paris: La Découverte, 2003)

—— *Psychoanalysis and Transversality: Texts and Interviews 1955–1971*, trans. by Ames Hodges (Los Angeles: Semiotext(e), 2015)

Guattari, Félix, and Danielle Sivadon, 'Le Préjugé démocratique. June 1987', *Chimères*, 94 (2019), pp. 144–48 <https://doi.org/10.3917/chime.094.0144>

Guerra, Carles, Joana Masó, Valérie Rousseau, and Edward Dioguardi, eds, *Francesc Tosquelles: Avant-Garde Psychiatry, Radical Politics, and Art* (New York: American Folk Art Museum, 2024)

'História da Biblioteca', Centro Hospitalar Psiquiátrico de Lisboa, n. d., <https://www.chpl.min-saude.pt/servicos-de-apoio-geral/biblioteca/historia/> [accessed 23 June 2024])

Izard, Georges, *L'Homme est révolutionnaire* (Paris: Grasset, 1945)

Jaspers, Karl, *General Psychopathology* [German original, 1913], trans. by J. Hoenig and Marian W. Hamilton (Baltimore, MD: John Hopkins University Press, 1997)

Kronfeld, Arthur, *Das Wesen der psychiatrischen Erkenntnis* (Berlin: Julius Springer, 1920)

Lacan, Jacques, 'Ce mercredi non jeudi 21.xi.63', *Magazine littéraire*, 304 (1992), p. 49

—— *De la psychose paranoïaque dans ses rapports avec la personnalité* [1932] (Paris: Seuil, 1975)

—— *Écrits: The First Complete Edition in English*, trans. by Bruce Fink in collaboration with Héloïse Fink and Russell Grigg (New York: W. W. Norton, 2006)

—— *Family Complexes in the Formation of the Individual* [French original, 1938], trans. by Cormac Gallagher (London: Karnac, 2003)

Lafont, Max, *L'Extermination douce. La Cause des fous, 40 000 malades mentaux morts de faim dans les hôpitaux sous Vichy* (Lormont: Le Bord de l'Eau, 2000)

Le Guillant, Louis, 'Introduction à une psychopathologie sociale', *L'Évolution psychiatrique*, 19.1 (1954), pp. 1–52

Lentz, Alexander K., 'Les Réflexes conditionnels salivaires chez l'homme sain et aliéné et leur rapprochement avec les données de la conscience', *L'Encéphale*, 30.2 (1935), pp. 394–440

Mabin, Dominique, and Renée Mabin, 'Art, folie et surréalisme à l'hôpital psychiatrique de Saint-Alban-sur-Limagnole pendant la guerre', *Mélusine*, 13 March 2015 <https://melusine-surrealisme.fr/wp/art-folie-et-surrealisme-a-lhopital-psychiatrique/> [accessed 30 March 2024]

Marx, Karl, '1) ad Feuerbach', in *Marx-Engels-Gesamtausgabe (MEGA^2)* (Berlin: Akademie Verlag), IV/3: *Exzerpte und Notizen. Sommer 1844 bis Anfang 1847* (1998), pp. 19–21

—— 'Economic and Philosophic Manuscripts of 1844', trans. by Martin Milligan and Dirk J. Struik, in *Marx & Engels Collected Works*, 50 vols (London: Lawrence and Wishart, 1975–2004), III: *Karl Marx: March 1843–August 1844*, digital edn (2010), pp. 229–346

—— *Karl Marx's Theses on Feuerbach: A New English Translation Based on the New Marx-Engels-Gesamtausgabe*, trans. by Carlos Bendaña-Pedroza, translation modified (2022) <https://www.academia.edu/42897184/Karl_Marx_s_Theses_on_Feuerbach_A_New_English_Translation_Based_on_the_New_Marx_Engels_Gesamtausgabe_By_Carlos_Bendaña_Pedroza> [accessed 8 April 2024]

—— 'Manuscrits économico-philosophiques de 1844', in *Œuvres philosophiques*, 54 vols (Paris: Éditions Costes, 1924–54), VI: *Économie allemande et philosophie, Idéologie allemande (1ère partie)*, trans. by Jules Molitor (1937)

—— 'Ökonomisch-philosophische Manuskripte (Erste Wiedergabe)', in *Marx-Engels-Gesamtausgabe (MEGA^2)* (Berlin: Dietz, 1975–), I/2: *Werke. Artikel. Entwürfe. März 1843 bis August 1844* (1982), pp. 187–322

—— 'Ökonomisch-philosophische Manuskripte aus dem Jahre 1844 (Zur Kritik der Nationalökonomie, mit einem Schlußkapitel über die Hegelsche Philosophie)', in *Marx-Engels-Gesamtausgabe (MEGA^1)*, 14 vols (Berlin: Marx-Engels-Verlag, 1927–40), I/3 (1932), pp. 29–172

—— '[Theses on Feuerbach]', trans. by the Institute of Marxism-Leninism, in *Marx & Engels Collected Works*, 50 vols (London: Lawrence and Wishart, 1975–2004), V: *Marx and Engels. 1845–1847* (1976), digital edn (2010), pp. 3–5

Masó, Joana, 'The Collective's Women', trans. by Perwana Nazif and Jesse Newberg, *Parapraxis*, 4 (August 2024)

Maublanc, René, 'Hegel et Marx', in *À la lumière du marxisme. Essais*, ed. by Henri Wallon and others (Paris: Éditions sociales internationales, 1935) pp. 189–232

Michaud, Ginette, *Laborde… un pari nécessaire. De la notion d'institution à la psychothérapie institutionnelle* (Paris: Gauthier-Villars/Bordas, 1977)

Mira y López, Emilio, *Psychiatry in War* (New York: W. W. Norton & Company, 1943) <https://www.miraylopez.com/PsW_tot.html> [accessed 3 April 2024]

Murard, Lion, and François Fourquet, eds, *Histoire de la psychiatrie de secteur ou le secteur impossible?*, special issue of *Recherches*, 17 (1975)

Naville, Pierre, *Psychologie, marxisme, matérialisme* [1946] (Paris: Rivière, 1948)

—— *La Psychologie, science du comportement: Le Béhaviorisme de Watson*, rev. edn (Paris: Gallimard, 1963)

Novaes, Clara, and Ana Carolina Patto, 'Félix et Jean. Des terrains vagues de la Garenne-Colombes à l'expérience de La Borde', *Chimères*, 102 (2023), pp. 129–42 <https://doi.org/10.3917/chime.102.0129>

Oury, Jean, *L'Aliénation* (Paris: Galilée, 1992)

Pain, François, 'Le Divan de Félix' [1986], chaosmosemedia, 2021 <https://chaosmosemedia.net/2021/05/25/le-divan-de-felix/> [accessed 7 April 2024]

Pavlov, Ivan, 'An Attempt at a Physiological Interpretation of Obsessional Neurosis and Paranoia', *Journal of Mental Science*, 80.329 (1934), pp. 187–97 <https://doi.org/10.1192/bjp.80.329.187-a>

—— 'Essai d'une interprétation physiologique de la paranoïa et de la névrose obsessionnelle', *L'Encéphale*, 30.2 (1935), pp. 381–93

Politzer, Georges, *Critique of the Foundations of Psychology: The Psychology of Psychoanalysis* [French original, 1928], trans. by Maurice Apprey (Pittsburgh, PA: Duquesne University Press, 1994)

—— 'Éditorial', *Revue de psychologie concrète*, 1 (1928), pp. 1–8

—— 'La Fin de la psychanalyse' [1939], in *Écrits 2. Les Fondements de la psychologie* (Paris: Éditions sociales,

1973)   <https://wikilivres.org/wiki/La_fin_de_la_ psychanalyse> [accessed 7 April 2024]

Reich, Wilhelm, 'Dialectical Materialism and Psychoanalysis' [1934], in *Sex-Pol: Essays, 1929–1934* (London and New York: Verso, 2012), pp. 1–74

—— 'The Masochistic Character' [German original, 1932], in *Character Analysis*, trans. by Vincent R. Carfagno and ed. by Mary Higgins and Chester M. Raphael (New York: Farrar, Straus and Giroux, 1980), pp. 225–69

Rorschach, Hermann, *Psychodiagnostics: A Diagnostic Test Based on Perception* [German original, 1921] (Bern: Hans Huber, 1942)

Roussy Gustave, and Michel Mosinger, 'Rapports anatomiques et physiologiques de l'hypothalamus et de l'hypophyse', *Annales de médecine*, 33.3 (1933), pp. 301–24

Tosquellas, Jacques, *Francesc Tosquelles. Psychiatre, catalan, marxiste* (Paris: Éditions d'une, 2019)

Tosquelles, Francesc, 'A Politics of Madness', trans. by Perwana Nasif, *Parapraxis*, 4 (August 2024)

Tosquelles, François, *Psychiatrie, psychanalyse et politique* (Paris: Éditions d'une, forthcoming)

—— *Psychopathologie et matérialisme dialectique* (Paris: Éditions d'une, 2019)

—— *Théorie et pratique de la psychothérapie institutionnelle*, 1982, in Tosquelles Archives, organized by Jacques Tosquellas

—— *Le Travail thérapeutique à l'hôpital psychiatrique* (Paris: Éditions du Scarabée, 1967)

—— *Le Travail thérapeutique en psychiatrie* [1967] (Toulouse: Érès, 2015)

—— *Le Vécu de la fin du monde dans la folie. Le Témoignage de Gérard de Nerval* (Grenoble: Jérôme Millon, 2012)

Wallon, Henri, *De l'acte à la pensée* (Paris: Flammarion, 1942)

—— 'Matérialisme dialectique et psychologie', in *Les Cours de l'université nouvelle. Cours de philosophie* (Paris: Éditions sociales, 1946), pp. 15–23

—— 'Science de la nature et science de l'homme: La Psychologie' [1931], *Enfance*, 12.3–4 (1959), pp. 203–19 <https:// doi.org/10.3406/enfan.1959.1435>

Wallon, Henri, and others, eds, 'Introduction', in *À la lumière du marxisme. Essais* (Paris: Éditions sociales internationales, 1935), pp. 9–16

Walter, Bernd, 'Hermann Simon — Psychiatriereformer, Sozial-
    darwinist, Nationalsozialist?', *Der Nervenarzt*, 73 (2002),
    pp. 1047–1054 <https://doi.org/10.1007/s00115-002-
    1431-z>

Notes on the Contributors

Steven Corcoran is a writer and translator living in Berlin. He has edited and/or translated several works by Jacques Rancière, including *Dissensus* (Continuum, 2010), two works by Alain Badiou, *Polemics* and *Conditions, Necropolitics* by Achille Mbembe, and *Alienation and Freedom* by Frantz Fanon (Bloomsbury, 2017).

Anthony Faramelli is a psychosocial theorist and practitioner. He is a lecturer in Visual Cultures at Goldsmiths, University of London. Faramelli is the author of *Resistance, Revolution and Fascism: Zapatismo and Assemblage Politics* and an editor of *Spaces of Crisis and Critique: Heterotopias Beyond Foucault* (both Bloomsbury Philosophy). Faramelli's research is focused on the theories and practices of institutional analysis.

Sophie Lesage is a researcher and editor. As the founder and principal editor of Éditions d'une, an independent publishing platform that emerged in 2014 from the work on the publication of the GTPSI proceedings (Groupe de travail de psychothérapie et de sociothérapie institutionnelles), she is committed to publishing foundational texts and recent scholarship in the field of institutional psychotherapy. Alongside key texts in the history of institutional psychotherapy, Éditions d'une has published scholarly discourse on the matter, including *Francesc Tosquelles. Psychiatre, catalan, marxiste*, ed. by Jacques Tosquellas, and *François Tosquelles et le travail*, ed. by Pascale Molinier.

Marlon Miguel is co-principal investigator of the project 'Madness, Media, Milieus: Reconfiguring the Humanities in Postwar Europe' at Bauhaus-Universität Weimar and visiting fellow at the ICI Berlin. He holds a double PhD in Fine Arts (Université Paris 8 Vincennes-Saint-Denis) and Philosophy (Federal University of Rio de Janeiro). His current research focuses on the intersection between contemporary philosophy, art, media, and psychiatry. He also practices contemporary circus and does practical movement research.

Jean Oury (1924–2014) was a French psychiatrist, psychoanalyst, and medical director of La Borde clinic. As a medical student in 1947, he attended the lecture series at École normale supérieure, in which Tosquelles's 'Psychopathology and Dialectical Materialism' was presented. Thereafter he decided to pursue psychiatry. Starting his career at Saint-Alban as an intern, he took part in the ongoing experiment of institutional psychotherapy. Oury completed his doctoral thesis, *Essai sur la conation esthétique* in 1950. His collaboration with Félix Guattari paved the way for founding La Borde clinic in 1953.

Christian Scheerhorn studied philosophy and comparative literature in Paris and Berlin. He is currently completing a Master's degree at Freie Universität Berlin with a research focus on the junctions of literature, media, and French philosophy. As a Student Research Assistant, he contributes to the project 'Madness, Media, Milieus: Reconfiguring the Humanities in Postwar Europe' at Bauhaus-Universität Weimar, exploring the history of institutional psychotherapy and its media and milieu practices.

François Tosquelles (1912–1994) was a Catalan physician, psychiatrist, psychoanalyst, co-founder of the POUM (Partit Obrer d'Unificació Marxista), and the institutional psychotherapy movement. In 1934 he was appointed as a physician in the Instituto Pere Mata in Reus and worked during the Spanish Civil War as psychiatric head of the Spanish Republican Army. After having spent three months at the concentration camp Septfonds, he found a way to the psychiatric clinic of Saint-Alban in Lozère. Tosquelles is author of a vast number of books, among them *Le Vécu de la fin du monde dans la folie. Le Témoignage de Gérard de Nerval, Le Travail thérapeutique à l'hôpital psychiatrique,* and *L'Enseignement de la folie.*

Elena Vogman is a scholar of comparative literature and media. She is principal investigator of the research project 'Madness, Media, Milieus: Reconfiguring the Humanities in Postwar Europe' at Bauhaus-Universität Weimar and visiting fellow at the ICI Berlin. She is the author of two books, *Sinnliches Denken. Eisensteins exzentrische Methode* (Diaphanes, 2018) and *Dance of Values: Sergei Eisenstein's Capital Project* (Diaphanes, 2019).

Index

Cultural Inquiry

EDITED BY CHRISTOPH F. E. HOLZHEY
AND MANUELE GRAGNOLATI